QUEER ADOLESCENCE

Understanding the Lives of Lesbian, Gay, Bisexual, Transgender, Queer, Intersex, and Asexual Youth

Charlie McNabb

ROWMAN & LITTLEFIELD

Lanham • Boulder • New York • London

Published by Rowman & Littlefield
An imprint of The Rowman & Littlefield Publishing Group, Inc.
4501 Forbes Boulevard, Suite 200, Lanham, Maryland 20706
www.rowman.com

86-90 Paul Street, London EC2A 4NE

British Library Cataloguing in Publication Information Available

Library of Congress Cataloging-in-Publication Data

Names: McNabb, Charlie, 1983– author.
Title: Queer adolescence : understanding the lives of lesbian, gay, bisexual, transgender, queer, intersex, and asexual youth / Charlie McNabb.
Description: Lanham : Rowman & Littlefield, [2020] | Includes bibliographical references and index. | Summary: "In this book, personal accounts mingle with factual information and sensitive analysis to provide a snapshot of the joys and concerns of lesbian, gay, bisexual, transgender, queer, intersex, and asexual adolescents."—Provided by publisher.
Identifiers: LCCN 2020013024 (print) | LCCN 2020013025 (ebook)
Subjects: LCSH: Gay youth. | Sexual minority youth. | Adolescence.
Classification: LCC HQ76.27.Y68 M36 2020 (print) | LCC HQ76.27.Y68 (ebook) | DDC 306.76/60835—dc23
LC record available at https://lccn.loc.gov/2020013024
LC ebook record available at https://lccn.loc.gov/2020013025

ISBN: 978-1-5381-3281-4 (cloth : alk. paper)
ISBN: 978-1-5381-9219-1 (pbk : alk. paper)
ISBN: 978-1-5381-3282-1 (ebook)

♾™ The paper used in this publication meets the minimum requirements of American National Standard for Information Sciences—Permanence of Paper for Printed Library Materials, ANSI/NISO Z39.48-1992.

To my love Erin, and to all queer youth
past, present, and future.

CONTENTS

FOREWORD

Charlie McNabb and I met as master's students in the folklore program at the University of Oregon, where we were both interested in research with queer populations. In the decade since, we've continued to pursue work and research that affirms queer identities. Over the years we've kept in touch, and Charlie helped me by providing feedback for a guide for teachers on working with LGBTQ+ youth and has spoken to my undergraduate folklore course on how folklore training informs their current work. I am delighted to see some of Charlie's important research on queer and transgender people in a book that can serve as a resource for queer youth as well as those who work with these populations. And by that, I mean all teachers and care providers, as we never know what identities the youth we work with may grow into.

In recent years LGBTQ+ people have become more visible, and social media is more prominently used among LGBTQ+ youth, causing some adults to have the mistaken assumption that youth do not need queer-inclusive curricula and care. But this is not the case, as young people still need guidance evaluating and finding accurate information about queer identities. They may also not have private internet access at home, or they may live in communities where queer people are only discussed in whispers, and never in a positive light. In the absence of mirrors[1] for their identity, queer students can feel lost as they navigate schooling, puberty, medical care, and all other typical adolescent experiences. This is even more important for those on "the margins of the margins"[2] or those who are outside of the gender binary, the more mainstream identities of lesbian and gay, and/or people of color. As a lesbian woman myself, I would like for more healthcare providers to be aware and intentionally inclusive of LGBTQ+ identities. This would save me from having to explain exactly why I do not need birth control, for example. The annoyances (and dangers) are more frequent for those outside of the gender binary, who may be denied even routine medical care by physicians who claim they do not know how to treat transgender patients.[3]

This book can provide a necessary mirror for adolescents who are queer, nonbinary, transgender, and asexual. As the participants in McNabb's study narrated, having representation in school and the media when they were young would have helped them realize their identities earlier and begin living a fuller life at a younger age. This is also true of more inclusive medical care, as some transgender and nonbinary adults (such as Seren in this volume) noted they wish they could have taken hormone blockers and received hormone replacement therapy (HRT) at puberty so their body would have developed in ways that better suited their gender identities. By sharing the narratives in this book with youth, teachers, parents, and care providers can allow questioning youth to see more possibilities for both their gender identity and their sexual orientation. Without these possible mirrors, it can be difficult to imagine a future outside of heteronormativity. Something like this would have benefited me as an adolescent; though I went to high school in a relatively liberal area of the country, I assumed I was straight because I did not see any alternatives. Compulsory heterosexuality[4] affects everyone and can be harmful to queer youth who are only presented with options of being in relationships with the "opposite sex." Youth who do not identify as a man or a woman at all, who identify differently from the gender they were assigned at birth, who do not desire a sexual or romantic relationship, and/or are not interested in heterosexual relationships need visible examples of the possibilities for different queer lives.

However, it is not only queer youth who benefit from the narratives and suggested actions within this book. Heterosexual and cisgender youth need windows into the lives of those who are different from them and sliding glass doors that allow them to visit these lives in their imaginations.[5] Books allow us to learn from and about others, and as the participants' voices are shared directly here, readers gain firsthand accounts from people with a variety of queer identities. As an English educator, I have witnessed how reading about a person outside of your community and experiences can have a profound effect on a reader. Many of my college students tell me they did not read, learn, or talk about queer experiences in their K–12 classes. Gaining exposure to queer differences earlier will be a benefit to everyone, as it allows these readers to recognize queer people they meet in life and have positive and accurate language to describe them, rather than slurs and stereotypes.

As I wrote when describing training for educators on queer issues, "There are many ways to be an advocate for queer students, but to go beyond inclusion and move into positive action, this advocacy must stem from knowledge of how society and our schools function within and through heteronormativity."[6] This book provides the necessary knowledge for action through McNabb's research with queer adults whose voices are missing from even queer-inclusive mainstream media, as well as the comprehensive suggestions that can apply to many care and service professions. In turn, their narratives can help all of us create more inclusive and welcoming spaces for youth. As an educator, I do not always know my students' identities, but I do not assume they are all (or even mostly) straight, cisgender, and allosexual. The stories in this volume can give me a reference point for students whose queer experiences are different from my own as a cisgender lesbian woman. Lastly, as a new parent, I hope that my child's future teachers and other caregivers will provide an open and inclusive environment so that children have multiple models for their future family life, not just one that includes an assumption that one must have a gender within the binary of male and female, have a romantic partner to be fulfilled, and only a partner that is of the "opposite sex." Teachers, medical professionals, and other youth service providers will benefit from reading this book and implementing and adapting the strategies for their particular work environments.

Summer Melody Pennell
PhD in Education
Assistant Professor of English Education, Truman State University
Author of *Queering Critical Literacy and Numeracy for Social Justice: Navigating the Course*

PREFACE

I began this research several years ago. At the time, I was investigating queer[1] and trans[2] menarche experiences—the first menstrual period. This is a fraught time in any youth's life, but particularly so when somebody who is decidedly not a woman is told, "You're a woman now!" or somebody with no interest in boys suddenly has new rules governing their access to male friends. More recently, I decided to open the research up to all queer and trans youths' experiences with adolescence in general. I realized that the entire life stage of adolescence can be challenging for any young person, but the added burden of figuring out one's non-normative sexuality or gender identity makes this period of time all the more confusing and frustrating. Queer youth have important stories to tell, and my hope is that this book can empower the newer generations of queer youth as well as help the adults in their lives to support them.

MY QUEER ADOLESCENCE

I was born in 1983 and grew up in a white upper-middle-class suburban household in Anchorage, Alaska. My gender questioning started early: When I was four years old, my parents gave me an age-appropriate talk about gendered genitals. I recall asking if there was any such thing as a "penis-vagina" because I was a "boygirl." They laughed indulgently and said no. From then until my late twenties, I suppressed that part of myself in an attempt to conform to familial and societal expectations.

Puberty itself was mostly typical, I think. Sex education was okay; it wasn't abstinence only but it also didn't mention queer people. Physically, menarche happened a bit early while breast development happened a bit late. I anxiously monitored these physiological changes and compared myself to my peers, like most young adolescents. Mood swings and confrontations with authority figures were perhaps a bit more antagonistic than normal; I was a bit of a terror to my mother.

When I was fourteen, I realized that the intense feelings I had had for certain childhood girl friends were actually crushes. I came out as bisexual[3] to my mother (my father had passed away by then); she was accepting but suggested that it might be a phase. I started attending a queer youth group outside of school called Stonewall Youth. I was fortunate to have this resource and it helped me learn about non-heterosexual and non-cisgender[4] identities and better understand my own identities. My mother stopped referring to my bisexuality as a phase and became very supportive. She even took pictures of my girlfriend and me for school dances. As it turned out, I realized I was a lesbian years later; for me, bisexuality was an exploratory period where I learned more about myself and who I loved and desired.

Midadolescence, through Stonewall Youth, I met a trans male teenager. I had never heard of this concept before and it blew me away. He was so self-assured and confident in his identity. I thought then that I might also be trans, but experimenting with "butching up"[5] did nothing to answer my questions. I slid back into girlhood. It wasn't until I was in my twenties that I learned about the concept of genderqueerness[6] or what today we mostly call nonbinary.[7] I remembered back to when I was four years old and telling my parents I was a boygirl and realized that I had always known who I was, but had simply suppressed it until I—and society—was more ready.

When I came out to my mother as nonbinary, she did not take it so well. She was confused and told me she would never use my "weird pronouns" (they/them)[8] or my chosen name. Like many parents, she softened over time and is now one of my biggest champions. I have been very lucky with my family's reaction; while some members have been perplexed, a few have started to use my pronouns and all now use my chosen (and now legal) name.

My transition[9] began in 2013 and is ongoing. I started by coming out to friends and presenting in more genderqueer ways, wearing a binder[10] and packer[11] while continuing to dress in traditionally feminine clothing. Then I legally changed my name and gender in court. When I changed my gender, there was no option for "nonbinary," so I just wrote it in. It worked, and very soon my state began offering an "X" gender marker on drivers' licenses. During this time, I also transitioned medically, starting low-dose testosterone and attaining a hysterectomy. At this point, I no longer bind or pack with any regularity, because my Autism makes me particularly sensitive to unusual physical sensations. I'm unsure whether my transition is complete or if I will go any further, and I am pursuing gender therapy to figure that out.[12]

Looking back over my adolescence, I think my experience was pretty average in many ways. There was a "girl code" at school where girls would give each other menstrual products as needed and whisper to tell each other if there was blood on someone's pants. There was fairly regular bullying about me being a nerd and then some rather overaggressive bullying about me being bisexual. I was physically and sexually assaulted by peers more than once for being queer. But I was never kicked out of my home, excommunicated from my church, or pushed into conversion therapy, like too many of my LGBTQIA+[13] peers.

I hope that these negative experiences become less typical as queer identities become more normalized through popular culture representation and youth coming out earlier. And I hope that more peers and adults become allies and learn to support the queer youth in their lives.

RESEARCH METHODS

I began with copious library and archival research. I read books on neurobiology and psychology; I analyzed data sets on queer youth homelessness and suicide. Then I administered a rather long survey to more than 150 people. Written informed consent was provided by each participant via a comprehensive informed consent question that was mandatory in order to continue the survey. The survey started with demographics questions and then went in depth into adolescence experiences, probing with open-ended questions. I was blown away by the participants' willingness to spend the time and emotional energy to

answer all those questions. After the survey ended, I chose ten participants for follow-up interviews. These interviews targeted specific experiences that each participant had discussed; for example, I followed up
on culturally specific identities, lesser-understood identities, and less
visible identities.

I utilized grounded theory to analyze data. After data collection, I
reviewed each survey and interview several times, noting repeated experiences, themes, and phrases. Then I made a list of codes from these
repeated ideas and went through the data, marking each time the idea
was mentioned. In secondary coding, I grouped the themes into categories. For more information on research methods, please visit https://
queeradolescence.com/research-methods.

STRUCTURE OF THE BOOK

The book begins with an introduction to the concepts of LGBTQIA+
and adolescence in chapter 1, "What Is Queer Adolescence?" Then, in
chapter 2, "Who We Are," you'll be introduced to the study participants. You'll get to know ten people from different walks of life and
learn about their queer adolescence experiences. There is also a big-
picture view of the demographics of the entire study group.

In chapter 3, "Sex Education," participants discuss their experiences
with formal and informal sexual education: how and what they learned
about their bodies, hygiene, sex, sexuality, and gender. Chapter 4, "Going through Puberty," recounts personal experiences of pubertal development, including physiological changes, gender and sexual identity
challenges, and what participants learned that wasn't covered in sex ed.

Chapter 5, "Parental and Peer Involvement," takes us in depth into
the kinds of supports these youth had growing up. Family, friends,
teachers, adult mentors, and peers all contributed—positively or negatively—to the adolescence experience.

Chapter 6, "Exploring Gender," is a discussion about gender identity
formation. Participants talk about how they learned about non-cisgender identities, their journeys realizing their own genders, and whether
they suppressed or celebrated their newfound identities. In chapter 7,
"Exploring Sexuality," participants discuss their journeys learning about
and exploring or suppressing their non-heterosexual sexual identities.

In chapter 8, "Coming Out," participants share whether, how, and to whom they came out, and what the reception was like. Chapter 9, "Transition," discusses participants' experiences with personal, social, medical, and legal transition.

Chapter 10, "What We Wish Had Been Different," is the longest and perhaps most important chapter. In it, participants reveal ideas about how they could have been supported in adolescence. These ideas are then organized into an action plan for parents, teachers, and clinicians to better support the queer youth in their lives. Although many of the experiences in this book were very difficult, this chapter offers a way forward.

The book ends with a helpful glossary and a list of recommended sex education resources for queer and trans youth and adults.

ACKNOWLEDGMENTS

I'd like to thank my wife, Erin, and the Bright Court Writing Retreat for allowing me the space and time to work on this project in peace and goodwill. I'd also like to thank my editors, Charles Harmon and Erinn Slanina, for their helpful advice on all things. Thanks to the copy editors and peer reviewers who strengthened this text immeasurably. Additionally, thanks to Zefyr Scott for his brilliant editing assistance with the survey text. Most of all, thank you to the participants of this study, who gave so much of themselves. Thank you for being vulnerable, honest, and candid with your experiences and feelings. This book would not exist without your solidarity and fearlessness.

I

WHAT IS QUEER ADOLESCENCE?

Adolescence can be a difficult time for youth. The conversations and silences around pubertal development in peer groups, family life, and the wider society can be awkward and confusing to negotiate. For LGBTQIA+ youth, the social and sexual challenges of puberty are frequently magnified. Often, queer youth are not just navigating developmental milestones, they are also coming to terms with their minoritized gender and/or sexual orientation statuses. This can mean substandard sex education experiences, interpersonal violence, homelessness, and identity repression. It can also mean deep resilience and pride.

WHO IS LGBTQIA+?

LGBTQIA+ is an acronym that intends to include all gender and sexual orientation minorities underneath a neat umbrella. It stands for lesbian, gay, bisexual, transgender, queer, intersex, asexual, and the "plus" signifies that there are myriad other identities that fit within this diverse group.

Lesbian

Lesbians are women or woman-aligned[1] people who are sexually or romantically attracted to other women or woman-aligned people. Some lesbians prefer to identify as gay or as gay women.

Gay

Gay can refer to men or man-aligned[2] people who are sexually or romantically attracted to other men or man-aligned people, or it can be a catchall for any same-sex feelings or behavior. For example, a lesbian or bisexual woman may refer to herself as gay.

Bisexual

Bisexuality can be a slippery concept. It can mean being sexually or romantically attracted to your own gender and another gender, being attracted to multiple genders, or being attracted to all genders. Some people believe that bisexuality means attraction just to women and men, preferring to use the related term "pansexual" to avoid excluding transgender people who may not fit neatly into the "man" or "woman" category. But transgender-inclusive bisexuals insist that bisexuality encompasses and includes trans people.

There are two popular stereotypes about bisexuals. One states that bisexuality is simply a stepping-stone on the way to accepting a 100 percent gay identity. The other posits that everybody is bisexual to some degree. Both of these falsehoods have been peddled by sex researchers. However, in the 1970s, when researchers began to talk to actual bisexuals, bisexuality was finally accepted as a valid identity.[3]

Transgender

Transgender people are those who identify as a different gender than the gender they were assigned at birth. This can include trans men, who were assigned female at birth; trans women, who were assigned male at birth; and nonbinary people, who identify as something other than the neat categories of "man" and "woman."

An older term, transsexual, specifically refers to those who have surgically transitioned or wish to. This positions gender identity in the genitals. Transgender, the more modern term, encompasses all who identify as another gender than that assigned at birth, regardless of transition status or goals.[4]

Queer

Queer is an inherently politicized identity as it is a reclaimed slur that reflects non-normativity, anti-assimilationism, and radical politics. Some people dislike the term due to its use as a derogatory word for same-gender-loving and transgender people. Some people prefer the term queer as they see other terms as too limiting or as having connotations that don't apply to them.[5] Other people use it as a catchall for all gender and sexual orientation minorities. In this book, "queer" will be used interchangeably with LGBTQIA+.

Intersex

Intersex people are those whose biological sex doesn't align strictly with the categories "male" or "female." This can include ambiguity or mixing of chromosomes, reproductive organs, sex hormones, external genitals, or secondary sex characteristics. Most intersex people are assigned a gender at birth, and most identify as that gender. Some do not and may identify as transgender.[6]

Asexual

Asexuality is a spectrum of sexual attraction from zero to some/occasional. Many asexuals are not sexually attracted to anybody. Some are slightly or occasionally attracted to some people, and are called gray-asexual. Some can be attracted to somebody, but only after the development of emotional attraction, and are called demisexual. Some may be sex-repulsed, while others may engage in partnered sexual activity in order to please a partner. Some experience no sexual libido while others do. "Asexual" is often shortened to "ace."[7]

Plus

The "plus" includes all gender and sexual orientation minorities who do not fit into the other categories. Some of these identities include culturally specific genders and orientations, such as Two-Spirit, which is a Native American, First Nations, or Alaska Native gender or sexual orientation; and hijra, which is an Indian third gender identity. Others differentiate more distinctly between sexual and romantic attraction; for example, somebody could be biromantic (romantically attracted to multiple genders) and asexual (not sexually attracted to anybody). Some people find that general terms such as "transgender" are too broad for them and prefer to identify more granularly as, for example, demigirl[8] or Autigender.[9] There are also people who are questioning or unsure of their gender or sexual orientation.

WHAT IS ADOLESCENCE?

Adolescence is a complex developmental phase with several factors. As a biological and social phenomenon, it can be defined by hormonal, physical, neurological, and behavioral changes. There is no precise age at which adolescence can be said to occur; it is a period of change that can occur between the ages of ten and twenty-four.[10] The term "adolescence" was coined relatively recently, by psychologist G. Stanley Hall in 1904. He defined it as a period of "storm and stress" involving conflict with authority figures and extreme mood swings.[11]

Developmental Milestones

Hormonally, there is a decrease in hypothalamus[12] and pituitary[13] sensitivity to estrogen[14] and testosterone;[15] an increase in luteinizing hormone[16] and follicle-stimulating hormone;[17] and, in people with ovaries, higher estrogen triggers gonadotropin-releasing hormone to initiate ovulation.[18]

These hormones cause several physical changes. In people with ovaries, the main changes are breast budding and subsequent growth, development of pubic and axillary[19] hair, a growth spurt, and the initiation of the menstrual cycle. These physical changes can take between one and a half and eight years to complete. In people with testes, the main changes are testicular enlargement and genital growth, development of pubic and axillary hair, a growth spurt, and sperm production and initiation of ejaculation. These physical changes can take between two and five years to complete.[20]

With pubertal development comes psychosocial change as well. One of the most important tasks for teenagers is achieving independence from their parents. This begins as a struggle, with behavioral problems such as rudeness and a decreased desire to follow rules and accept parental advice. Once independence is achieved, however, the adolescent then integrates back into the family and once again accepts parental guidance. [21]

Adolescents also become highly aware of and concerned with their bodies. In early adolescence (ages ten to thirteen), youth are uncertain and anxious about their bodies and frequently compare them to their peers' bodies. In middle adolescence (ages fourteen to sixteen), most adolescents have ended or nearly ended pubertal changes and become increasingly anxious about weight; some develop eating disorders during this time. By late adolescence (ages seventeen to twenty-one), most adolescents are unconcerned with body image unless there has been abnormal development. [22]

In early and middle adolescence, youth tend to become very close with their peer groups. As they separate from family involvement, they become highly dependent on peers; first socializing mostly with the same sex and conforming to group codes and dress, then beginning to date and explore sexually. In late adolescence, youth have generally established their own values and no longer succumb to peer pressure. They are also often more interested in romantic partnering than in group activities. [23]

Finally, adolescence involves intense identity development. In early adolescence, youth begin to develop new cognitive abilities such as abstract reasoning. [24] They begin to set future goals and develop personal values. They also tend to begin to experience sexual feelings, an increased need for privacy, and the need for immediate gratification. In middle adolescence, intellectual and creative abilities increase, as do emotional awareness and openness. Youth become less idealistic and more likely to exhibit risk-taking behaviors such as substance use. In late adolescence, youth become more rational and realistic, develop a sense of perspective, and expand their moral and sexual values. [25]

Some theorists (namely, Jeffrey Arnett) posit another stage of life between adolescence and adulthood, termed "emerging adulthood." This phase is "distinguished by relative independence from social roles and from normative expectations." [26] Emerging adults have the freedom to explore many possible identities and values in love, work, and worldview. This life stage is possible only in industrialized or postindustrial societies where marriage and parenthood come later in life and more people pursue higher education.[27]

Sexual Identity

For allosexuals,[28] sexual behavior begins with preadolescent curiosity and masturbation. In early adolescence, pubertal development triggers intense body curiosity, sexual fantasizing, and masturbation in response to sexual feelings. In middle adolescence, youth begin more exploratory, experimental sexual behavior; may begin dating and partnered sexual activity; and typically display little concern for sexual risks. In late adolescence, youth develop more expressive sexual behavior and may develop intimate relationships.[29]

Eric Meininger and Gary Remafedi posit four stages to acquire a lesbian, gay, or bisexual identity. In stage I, sensitization, a child has the sense of feeling different from peers; there may be same-sex feelings and behaviors. In stage II, identity confusion, the adolescent identifies feelings and behaviors as homosexual and experiences further isolation and a feeling of difference. In stage III, identity assumption, the individual adopts the gay, lesbian, or bisexual identity and may disclose it to others. In stage IV, commitment, the individual fully accepts their identity and no longer wants to be straight to fit in.[30] Models like this position the final stage as being mature and "done" with the trajectory, while some individuals may never reach that final stage or may skip or repeat other stages.

Some researchers have suggested that sexual orientation is fixed in the brain in utero and is activated during puberty.[31] Youth generally become aware of same-sex attraction around the same time that heterosexual youth develop sexual interests, between about ten and fifteen years old. Identity assumption occurs at the end of this phase, and coming out is often delayed another year, or around sixteen years of age, though it is often delayed much longer if the individual perceives risk in coming out.[32] Models like this allow for delaying coming out but don't account for those individuals who never come out, either because of safety risks or because they do not see a need.

Dena Phillips Swanson, Malik Chaka Edwards, and Margaret Beale Spencer have suggested a simpler model for sexual identity development: first, initial awareness of same-sex attraction; second, first sexual contact; and third, disclosure to self and others.[33] Of course, this doesn't account for those queer youth who hold off on sexual relationships but still have self-awareness of and disclose their queerness.

Other researchers disagree with these models as well: "Stage models tend to reify and simplify transitions in our lives, which are actually much more complex and occur over time."[34] For example, many queer youth go through a phase of heterosexual experimenting before settling on a queer identity. On the other hand, many have realized they are queer before any sexual experimentation. These dominant narratives may be a response to the emerging queer political movement; some folks feel pressured to assimilate to a normative identity with a normative history. However, queer adults report many different paths into self-awareness and self-disclosure that do not necessarily follow the neat path of a given stage model.[35]

I believe that these models have value as theories of a normative path, but it's important to recognize that not everybody's path is normative, that many people skip stages or take them out of order, and that many people do not reach the end of the path. All paths are still valid.

Asexuals often have a longer path to sexual identity formation. Only recently have there been public, organized asexual groups, and they can still be difficult to locate and access. Many asexuals come out later than gays, lesbians, and bisexuals simply because they have no group to identify with and learn about themselves. Self-labeling generally occurs before disclosing to others.[36] Before finding such resources, asexuals often find themselves confused and alienated as popular culture portrays adolescents as being sex-obsessed and most of their peers do develop sexual attractions to others.[37]

Gender Identity

Gender identity is a person's internal sense of being male, female, or nonbinary.[38] Children tend to know their own gender by the age of four. Although many transgender children are aware of their transgender status, they are also highly aware of the threat of rejection for disclosing it. Many take care to fully learn the stereotypical behaviors associated with their assigned gender and perform their assigned gender in order to avoid being rejected by their families and the wider society. Others have a sense of being different or feeling wrong, but don't fully realize they are transgender until later, in adolescence or adulthood.[39]

Gender identity formation does not have the breadth of research that sexual identity formation does. Aaron Devor's fourteen-stage model is perhaps the most comprehensive transgender identity formation model at this time. In stage 1, the individual experiences unfocused anxiety about their gender. In stage 2, the individual has identity confusion and doubts about their assigned gender and performs reactive gender-conforming behaviors. Stage 3 involves comparing the assigned gender with the felt gender and experimentation with alternative gender consistent roles.[40]

In stage 4, the individual discovers the concept of transsexuality or transgenderism.[41] Then, in stage 5, they experience doubts about their own gender and seek more information about trans identities. Stage 6 has the individual testing their possible trans identity and beginning to disidentify with their assigned gender. In stage 7, they become more tolerant of their probable trans identity and increasingly disidentify with their assigned gender.[42]

Stage 8 involves seeking more information and confirmation of the individual's trans identity, as well as reality testing[43] in intimate relationships. In stage 9, the individual fully accepts their trans identity and comes out to others. In stage 10, there is a delay before transition as the individual learns about transition options and begins to socialize as their true gender.[44]

In stage 11, the individual transitions through legal, medical, and/or surgical means. Stage 12 has the individual living successfully post-transition and accepting their post-transition gender identity. In stage 13, the individual focuses on identity integration and stigma management; their trans identity is mostly nonvisible. Finally, in stage 14, the individual feels pride about their trans identity and may engage in trans advocacy.[45]

Many transgender people do not follow this entire path. For one, many trans people do not transition, either because they do not wish to, because they cannot afford to, or because of medical gatekeeping.[46] Also, some trans people want to be stealth: living as their affirmed gender and not discussing or admitting their trans experience to others. Devor does acknowledge this:

> [A]ny person may enter into a process which resembles the one outlined here but may conclude that the best way for them to live their lives is to go no further than any particular stage. Just because an individual may seem to be following the trajectory described herein does not mean that they will end up making any particular choice for any particular outcome. This model is only intended to provide some insights into a commonly followed path. It is by no means the only path, nor will all who appear to be following it come to the same conclusions. [47]

This model is rather lengthy and not all individuals follow it completely. Some may skip steps, stop early, or move through the steps out of order. This does not make them less mature or invalidate their trans identities.

Another, briefer transgender identity development theory by Heidi M. Levitt and Maria R. Ippolito presents three "clusters" of common experiences rather than positing a stage model. The first cluster, "From Childhood Treated Like Damaged Goods," describes the relentless burden to conform to cisgender standards. Many participants reported hiding their true gender and experiencing self-loathing and isolation. Sometimes, cross-gender behavior was policed via bullying, alienation, and even physical violence. [48]

The second cluster, "The Power of Language in Fostering Acceptance," reveals that being exposed to positive transgender narratives allows individuals to expand their own self-exploration. Many participants described affirming spaces such as LGBTQIA+ groups as being lifesaving. Being in community also gave participants the opportunity to learn and play with gender labels, which could be validating. [49]

The third cluster, "Identity Formation Is an Ongoing Process of Balancing Authenticity and Necessity," describes participants' gender identity formation as an ongoing process, with sometimes unexpected or surprising shifts. Gender transition, for example, can also cause a shift in sexual orientation. Additionally, while individuals negotiate their feelings of authenticity in their gender, they also must consider things like financial stability and physical safety. [50]

This theory was formed through a grounded theory approach much like the approach I use in my own research. Therefore, it offers only one possible interpretation of the data. Additionally, like all human subject research, it is limited to the participants involved, who in this case were mostly white and from a Christian background. Still, these

clusters are intriguing and may be useful for scholars researching transgender identity development.

Coming Out

Coming out is the process of disclosing one's non-heterosexual or non-
cisgender identity to oneself and the people in one's life. It can happen
at any time in the life span and often is a continual process over an
individual's life, as heterosexuality and cisgender status are recognized
as normative and thus expected. Because coming out can occur during
adolescence, I include information here.

In the past, most young people waited to disclose their sexual and
gender identities until after leaving home (and sometimes much later)
to avoid familial rejection, forced homelessness, and the threat of physical violence. However, with gender and sexual orientation minorities
becoming more mainstream in popular culture, societal acceptance has
risen and many youth are coming out earlier, in early and middle adolescence.[51]

Furthermore, the age of social networking has allowed many adolescents access to other queer peers and mentors through blogging, forums, video sharing, chat services, and other social media. Queer narratives are often more accessible, and youth have more freedom to explore new and emerging identities while remaining assigned gender- or
heterosexual-conforming in real life. Many queer youth come out first
via the internet to friends who may be purely online friends, rather than
IRL (in real life) friends. Still, they often have to navigate homophobic
and transphobic messages on the internet.[52]

When youth do choose to come out, they must do a risk assessment
for financial, social, and physical safety. They have to think about the
values and behaviors of their families, religious communities, peers,
school communities, and the wider societal context. Often, they disclose
to a trusted friend or sibling first. If they determine that their environment is too risky to come out in, they often suppress their gender or
sexual identity to fit in and remain safe.[53] It's a catch-22 for youth: If
they come out, they may face discrimination or violence, but if they
remain closeted, they may experience alienation, isolation, and other
psychological issues.[54]

There are several stages to coming out. First, identity confusion or awareness of being different, sometimes with feelings of guilt. Then, identity comparison or seeing their identity through a homophobic or transphobic lens, sometimes with feelings of panic at being "inferior." In the identity tolerance stage, the individual questions the majority view and determines that society, rather than the individual, is "wrong." Next, identity acceptance brings complete acceptance of the identity and initiates coming out. Then, identity pride occurs, wherein the individual immerses themself into the queer community. Finally, in the identity synthesis stage, the individual realizes that being queer is just one of many identities and feels less vulnerable to homophobia and transphobia.[55] Of course, as above, stage models can be flawed since not all individuals decide to come out at all and those who do may follow a different path. Still, this model can be useful for understanding a typical path for self-acceptance and disclosure.

2

WHO WE ARE

This study looks at the adolescence experiences of LGBTQIA+ people. These youth often have a more challenging adolescence, as they are not just contending with pubertal and social changes but are also coming to terms with their minoritized gender and/or sexual orientation statuses.

The participants in this study were numerous and fairly diverse. A total of 153 people responded to the long survey, of which 150 fit the inclusion criteria. These 150 people shared about their lives with vulnerability and candor. Then I chose ten for follow-up interviews, based on their willingness and my desire to capture a deeper snapshot of participant diversity. In this chapter, I introduce each interviewee with a brief biographical vignette, then discuss the overall demographics of the participants.

INTERVIEWEES

Participants selected their preferred form of identification at the beginning of the survey. Some wanted to use their first name or a pseudonym of their choice, while others chose to allow me to identify them with letters of the alphabet. Christina, Joe, Lane, RK, Seren, Skylar, T, Tommie Jayne, V, and X participated in follow-up interviews and are introduced here.

Christina

> *It's a planned puberty, and I am using the internet as a resource to monitor my own pubescence, so logistically very different, of course. I'm very aware of the changes in my body, as opposed to my first puberty which I was more aware of the external world. The fact that I'm feeling some emotional relief through HRT is making puberty seem "awesome," so far. I know my body needs to go through changes, and I know it's going to be rough sometimes, so I'm able to get through the painful parts and appreciate the wonderful easier parts.*—Christina, discussing how second puberty has differed from natal puberty

Christina is a Filipino transgender woman who identifies as pansexual[1] and demisexual.[2] She was born in 1975 and grew up middle class in Oregon, Hawaii, California, New York, and Kansas, in suburban neighborhoods as well as military bases.

Her sex education was minimal to none, with no information or resources about sexual orientation or gender identity. Her parents and peers were overall unsupportive and her pubertal experiences were surprising and unnerving, as she had very little knowledge of what was normal and what might happen.

Christina's gender journey started in high school; she loved wearing dresses and makeup but was deeply ashamed and told nobody. She started dressing up for Halloween every year as a way to let herself be free and to test her peers. Everybody would laugh, finding it funny. She remained closeted until she was forty-two years old.

She socially transitioned at home, and gradually her family grew to accept her. Then she came out publicly, got a new job, and started hormone replacement therapy. For the first time in her life, she feels calm and free, happy with her gender. She considers herself Māhū, which translates roughly to "between genders." This culturally specific gender identity affects her interpretations of masculinity and femininity; she rejects American cultural norms that demand a gender binary.

When asked what she wishes had been different about her adolescence, Christina responded, "Supportive parents and community. Honesty about sex and gender. Less stigma."

Joe

The term "gay" was the first queer word I heard and there was nothing positive about it. It was used to express people's disinterest in an activity or to emasculate boys. Having no vocabulary or representation for what I was experiencing, I quickly internalized a lot of the negativity surrounding being "gay," filling up with shame and self-hatred which resulted in a deep depression and my first suicide attempt by halfway through the 7th grade.—Joe, talking about their early understandings of sexuality

Joe is a white genderqueer person who identifies as queer. They were born in 1990 and grew up working class in a suburban neighborhood in Washington state.

Their sex education was mostly focused on sexually transmitted infections and the process of pregnancy and birth: "Many of us walked away feeling like sex was either bad or that we simply wanted to avoid all the negative outcomes, but there was no information provided on what sex was, least of all how to avoid it." Joe learned very little about sexuality before they were eighteen years old and free to explore on their own. What they did learn was that heterosexuality was the default and anything other than that was inferior.

Puberty was fairly uneventful, but Joe had issues with their periods that they now realize was minor dysphoria, as well as discomfort and embarrassment due to societal silence and shaming around menstruation. Parental involvement was limited to hygiene suggestions. Peer involvement, on the other hand, was largely negative, and included body and gender policing as well as the aforementioned mockery of any hint of queerness.

When they were eight years old, Joe saw the movie *Mulan*, which portrays a young woman dressing as a man to escape strict gender roles. It was Joe's first time relating to a character in that way; they were finally able to articulate that gender roles were suffocating them and that they identified somewhere in between male and female. However, these thoughts were suppressed in order to fit in to a cruel school community.

In their mid-twenties, Joe found the space to explore their gender identity more fully and began to transition. They stopped their periods with a hormonal intrauterine device (IUD), started more often going by their masculine nickname, started using they/them pronouns, and began wearing men's clothing and refraining from shaving body hair. These changes have been validating and mean a lot for their well-being.

In terms of sexuality, Joe discovered an attraction to girls in seventh grade and felt ashamed. They suppressed their queerness until they were eighteen years old and attended their first Pride celebration. Seeing so many people openly showing affection for each other was a mind-opening opportunity, and Joe realized that they could have that too. After this experience, they came out informally by changing their sexual orientation on their social media profiles to bisexual.

When thinking back to their adolescence, Joe wishes that they had known someone else like them. They also would have wanted better sex education that included comprehensive anatomy lessons, discussion of safe sex and consent, and queer content. For youth today, they suggest that there should be more resources available at earlier ages. Younger children should see queer relationships in texts; preteens and teens should see representation of characters struggling with or developing their gender or sexual identities. Importantly, books should have innocuous titles to protect those youth living with parents or caretakers who might disagree with their reading queer content.

Lane

> I had two or three teachers that were very supportive of me and my coming-out experience. I had a creative writing teacher who always used my preferred name when calling roll and always used they/them pronouns when referring to me, and did it really naturally, not calling it out. He also disciplined the jocks when they made fun of my pronouns. He would redirect them right away toward talking about something else. He'd call it out right away instead of waiting until after class to talk to them.—Lane, talking about the importance of supportive teachers

Lane is a white nonbinary person who identifies as pansexual. They were born in 1999 and grew up working class in a small town in Wisconsin.

Their sex education in school was separated by sex and focused on puberty and sexually transmitted diseases in a heteronormative context.

Lane learned about sexual orientation and gender identity in their Gay-Straight Alliance (GSA) in high school but were forced to stop attending when their father suggested the group was "turning them gay."

Puberty was rough for Lane. They started puberty early and felt immediate and intense dysphoria about breast development. They hated their body and had a difficult time with swim team because of the tight and high-rising competition suit. Parental involvement was minimal; their stepsister taught them how to shave their legs and their stepmother told them about menstruation. Their father had to force them to wear a bra to cover their developing chest. Peer involvement was more negative, involving gender and body policing: People were judgmental about their body hair.

Lane's gender journey started at age nine when they started puberty and developed gender dysphoria. In the GSA, they learned about transgender identities and thought that perhaps they were a trans man. They bought a binder and cut their hair short. Their father was initially unsupportive, and they went back into the closet until they were twenty years old. They discovered their nonbinary identity through social media education and support, came out, and began transition. They chose not to do hormone replacement therapy, but are pursuing top surgery.

In high school, Lane realized they are pansexual. They are attracted to energy and personality; gender doesn't matter to them. They hid their queer feelings until they fell for a teammate. Their father was accepting, but wanted them to abstain from publicly showing affection in front of conservative or younger family members. Their younger brother and high school teachers were their biggest supports in high school. They now have a partner of two years who loves and accepts them.

Lane has several wishes for their ideal adolescence: They wish their father had been more accepting and had helped them be their true self, they wish they had not been raised in an abusive stepfamily home, and they wish they had been raised more neutrally rather than with enforced femininity. In thinking about the younger generation of queer youth, Lane wishes that teachers would incorporate LGBTQIA+ topics into the curriculum. History class, for example, would be a great class to include queer history. Additionally, they think that schools should have posters for queer hotlines and information websites in libraries and resource centers.

RK

> *People are just baffled or can't even imagine how an otherwise nor-*
> *mal mandudeguybro just doesn't experience sexual attraction. It's*
> *like sexual attraction is such an ingrained part of masculinity that*
> *they can't fathom the two as separate. Then there's explaining asexu-*
> *ality to hostile Queer folx, who're often so deep in the most toxic*
> *Tumblr drama and B.S. that they can't even have a conversation with*
> *a real person from outside that warped lens.*—RK, discussing how
> asexuality is a poorly understood orientation

RK is a white cisgender man who identifies as asexual and biromantic.[3]
He was born in 1990 and grew up upper middle class in a suburban
neighborhood in California.

He had fairly comprehensive sex education in school and at home.
In seventh grade, he learned about anatomy, pregnancy basics, sexually
transmitted infections, and contraception methods. Then in high
school, there were two more units: one that covered anatomy, pregnancy, and sexually transmitted infections in greater detail and one that
discussed relationships and emotional aspects of sexuality. Queer identities were briefly mentioned. At home, RK's parents gave him age-
appropriate books and encouraged him to ask questions. Most of the
practical aspects of puberty and sexuality he learned by himself or
through friends and the internet.

RK says his puberty was typical; vocal development and body hair
were slightly earlier than others in his grade due to his being a bit older.
He enjoyed the extra muscle development and was proud of his body
hair. Emotionally, he sometimes felt unfulfilled or angry: "I easily fell
into the surly teen trope, but instead of rebelling through sex and alco-
hol I chose mountain biking and simply not coming home for dinner."

His parents were supportive, although he was trying to achieve emotional independence and therefore didn't take them up on their offers
for guidance. Peers were supportive and he had queer people at school
to talk to.

RK began developing his sexual identity in fourth grade, when he
got a crush on another boy. He got a crush on a girl not long after, so he
knew he wasn't straight, but not fully gay either. He learned about
bisexuality via an encyclopedia in the classroom and decided that label

fit him at the time. In high school, he came out as bisexual, and received good support from family and friends.

In his later teens, RK didn't understand what all the fuss was about around sex. He experimented with hooking up with men and women and just didn't understand what he was missing. At some point he googled "why don't I want to have sex" and finally learned about asexuality at the age of twenty-one. After realizing he was asexual, he came out again, and that coming out experience was totally different. Asexuality is still a misunderstood or even invisible sexual orientation to most people. Because of the lack of ace visibility, RK feels obligated to be visible in a way he never had to when he thought he was bisexual.

While RK had a typical puberty and feels that adolescence is supposed to be a bit messy, he does wish that sex education classes went over LGBTQIA+ experiences more in depth, and he thinks things might have been easier for him if he'd known about the asexuality spectrum earlier. When asked about asexual resources, he said that there aren't enough, and books written about asexuality by non-asexuals are often problematic. Because the asexual spectrum and the concept of libido versus desire are complex, RK thinks the best way to share these ideas is in a resource packet to give youth time to explore on their own schedule and level of understanding.

Seren

> Being neuroatypical,[4] being already marked "weird," opens me up to self-analysis. I don't think necessarily you're more likely to be not-cisgender if you're neuroatypical, but being othered, you're already observing something that others dismiss or simplify. You're more prone to questioning. I would say it doesn't inform my gender identity, but it did empower me to find it, it made me as a neuroatypical person more likely to enter into self-discovery.—Seren, discussing how Autism impacts her gender identity

Seren is a white nonbinary transgender woman who identifies as lesbian, queer, and asexual. She was born in 1987 and grew up middle class in suburban neighborhoods in Oklahoma and Oregon.

Sex education was abstinence-only and overly vague. Seren remembers having to look at photographs of sexually transmitted infections that had progressed very far without treatment, and an abstinence rally in middle school facilitated by the high schoolers. There was a video about "wetting the bed" that she didn't realize was about nocturnal emissions for years. Fear tactics and euphemisms, she says, just further stigmatized the idea of honest discussions.

Puberty was full of shame. Seren had severe acne and serious dysphoria about her leg and facial hair. She never wanted people to see her legs or to take pictures of her in harsh light, where her stubble and acne were more noticeable. Parental support was minimal, as she didn't know she was supposed to ask her family questions, and they didn't spontaneously offer answers. Peer involvement was negative: "Sometimes I heard them say things about other people, and that's how I learned what I should or shouldn't try to do."

As Seren reached young adulthood, people began to refer to her as a "young man," which felt wrong to her. She didn't understand what "man" meant and only knew that it didn't fit her. As she physically changed through puberty, the hairiness and musculature made her uneasy and she thought she was ugly. In college, she was exposed to the term "gender nonconforming" and decided that it fit her. Over time, she met nonconforming men and realized she didn't really identify in that way. Finally, she realized that she was a genderqueer woman. She changed her legal documentation and began the process of permanent facial hair removal and started hormone replacement therapy. Second puberty has been amazing: "I'm going forward in life knowing who I am and knowing what my goals are and happy to finally be the person I want to be."

Her sexual identity formed later in life. She spent so much energy early on just trying to belong that she didn't really have time to consider her sexuality. When she started college, she was exposed to non-heterosexual people for the first time, and began to consider who she was in relation to heterosexuality or queerness. Only recently, with her realization of her feminine identity, has she come to understand that she's an asexual lesbian. She also uses the terms "gay" and "queer." Seren came out in her late twenties and early thirties. She slowly uncovered layers for her parents, and was just as open as she could be with friends.

When asked about her ideal adolescence, Seren had a lot of ideas. First, school sex education should have included information about consent, negotiating pleasure, and actual facts instead of scare tactics. Also, she wishes she had been exposed to ideas about gender and sexuality at a much younger age. Finally, she would have much preferred to start transitioning earlier in life, before testosterone made so many permanent changes to her body, and to have a close mother-daughter relationship with her mother.

Skylar

My parents and peers kept reinforcing that I was supposed to be uncomfortable, as a default, and I didn't understand that wanting to crawl out of my skin because of my assigned gender wasn't normal. I shaved only because it was expected of me, even though it took a lot of time and effort, and it caused me anxiety.—Skylar, talking about parent and peer involvement during puberty

Skylar is a white Hispanic neutrois[5] person who identifies as biromantic and demisexual. He was born in 1994 and grew up upper class in a suburban neighborhood in Washington state.

He did not receive a formal sex education and grew up in an evangelical church, where the only options were being cisgender and heterosexual. He didn't feel able to be curious about sex and only learned about gender identity and sexual orientation at the end of middle school via social media networks.

Puberty was extremely uncomfortable. Initially, Skylar attempted to dress in a more masculine way, but when pubertal development continued, he grudgingly accepted his assigned sex and tried to do all the "right" things. Parental and peer involvement was minimal and mostly focused on policing his gender presentation.

When he was three years old, Skylar told his mother that he looked like his father, and she vehemently disagreed. So he hid that part of him for years. Only after much scrolling on deviantart, fanfiction.net, and Tumblr did he grow to understand his gender. He started out as a consumer but then, after realizing he was trans, started producing queer content on these platforms. He came out at age nineteen, in his first year living out of his parents' house, and immediately began living authentically. He obtained top surgery, legally changed his name, and transitioned socially so his presentation matches how he feels internally.

Sexual identity development was somewhat slower. Being Autistic, he didn't recognize that his intense friendships were actually crushes. Again, through social media, he grew to understand his sexuality. At the time, he identified as a girl, so recognizing his obsessions with girls clued him in that he wasn't straight. Now that he's accepted his gender identity, he's more attracted to men. He came out as biromantic and demisexual at age twenty.

When he looks back to his adolescence, Skylar wishes that he had had more support and options to explore without fear of judgment or prejudice. For the younger generations of queer adolescents, he wishes that sex education wasn't a single-day topic and that the language was more inclusive of queer and trans people. Finally, he says that queer content should be talked about in ways that aren't inherently politicized.

T

Mental and medical health providers should do their own research and/or attend conferences, reach out to learn from other trans people or allies that advocate for trans people and provide education. Clients/patients should not be responsible for educating.—T, discussing his frustrations with incompetent providers

T is a white transgender man who identifies as straight. He was born in 1990 and grew up upper middle class in suburban neighborhoods in Illinois, Ohio, and Alabama.

For T, sex education was dismal. His family didn't tell him anything regarding puberty or sexuality. Formal school sex education was very cis-heteronormative and biased. Puberty was an awful experience; he hated his body and was depressed and suicidal. There was no support from family, peers, or the wider community.

He was confused about gender for a long time; he felt like a man but didn't know the concept of transgender identities. In his twenties, T finally ran across the word "transgender" on social media and came to understand his gender identity. He came out later in life, when he was financially stable, in case his parents disowned him.

Transition has been very difficult, with little support from anybody. Still, he ably navigated social, medical, and legal transition on his own.

Learning about transition options was largely word-of-mouth. He learned about top surgery from an Instagram post. The man from the account told him about informed consent clinics, and he was able to find one in his city. Then, at that clinic, he met another transgender man and learned about more resources.

Besides competent medical providers, T wishes that somebody could have helped him during his adolescence. It would have been beneficial if somebody had known what was going on with him and educated him about transgender identities so that he could have transitioned sooner and experienced less distress.

Tommie Jayne

> *I didn't know that I wasn't supposed to be a girl until the day before my sister's first birthday party. I wasn't quite four and was expecting to get my hair curled and my cousin's pink dress to wear. Instead, I was taken for my first of countless buzz cuts and dressed up in a really stupid-looking sailor suit. My parents refused to listen to any of my complaints, and they were hitters, so I shut up quickly and played along as best I could.*—Tommie Jayne, talking about early gender suppression

Tommie Jayne is a Native American Two-Spirit intersex person who identifies as heterosexual. She was born in 1954 and grew up upper middle class in an urban neighborhood in Illinois. She was subjected to genital surgery as a toddler, leaving her with an overactive penis and a brain that can't see it properly.

Her first sex education lesson came from her parents informing her that girls didn't have penises and boys only cried when they bleed at about age four. They explained the process of heterosexual sex to her at an early age and then never talked about it again.

Puberty was a nightmare for Tommie Jayne. Her physique was very feminine and puberty came late, so she was bullied in the high school locker rooms. She masturbated frequently to cope with gender dysphoria. She says, "I made my deal with spirit young and just resolved to take it as it came and play male as best as I could." Her parents were abusive, and she went to live with her aunt in high school.

While she knew that she was a girl from a young age, she suppressed her identity due to abuse. She was caught crossdressing twice and punished severely, so she stopped doing that and hid behind a beard and grungy clothes for years. She finally came out in 2010 and began transitioning in 2014. The biggest change for her was not being self-conscious about how she moved, posed, or spoke. She could finally be herself and not pretend to be male. She says that hormone replacement therapy has made her feel peaceful and comfortable at last.

For Tommie Jayne, an ideal adolescence would be to have had what she sees trans kids experiencing now. She wishes that she had been raised like Jazz Jennings in a supportive family with early access to transition options. She also thinks that there should be better indexing of transgender resources, so that they are more easily discoverable.

V

I always knew I was queer, just didn't know how due to presenting as the wrong gender my whole life. Turns out once I had a good sense of who I was and my correct gender, I don't feel a compulsory attraction to men to feel more feminine. I am a woman, and I love women!—V, discussing her sexuality journey

V is a biracial (Armenian/Anglo) transgender woman who identifies as a lesbian. She was born in 1991 and grew up lower middle class in a rural area in Massachusetts.

V's school sex education was decent but cis-heteronormative. She didn't learn much from family. Puberty was confusing, and she experienced dysphoria with her body masculinizing. Sexuality was confusing without a solid idea of her gender identity. Parental involvement was very low, and V felt pressure to conform to her gender assigned at birth due to social norms that heightened during puberty.

She had no idea about transgender identities until college, which set her back in terms of figuring out her gender identity. Because of poor media representation, she thought that trans women were men in dresses, and had never heard of trans men or nonbinary people. She learned the truth about transgender identities and transitioning through online resources and forums.

Fairly recently, V's dysphoria finally won out over her anxiety and she decided to start the process of transitioning. She just started hormone replacement therapy and has some surgical procedures scheduled. Being a woman was always something that would be amazing, and now she's finally achieving her dream.

When reflecting about her adolescence, V says that she would have liked to be educated about trans issues and learned about hormone replacement therapy before becoming an adult and passing the age when medical transition produces the best results. She has a lot of regret and anger that it took her so long to realize her identity. In terms of the younger queer and trans generations, V wants gender and sexuality resources to expand outside the more targeted programs: "It definitely pains me to see people who have all these feelings about their sexuality and gender without knowing anyone else can relate."

X

I came out to my gay family friend and he advised me to come out to my mom before I went off to college. So in my late 17th year of being alive, I told my mom and she had a great many questions that were only slightly annoying and in my best interest. She voiced that she wished for me to be straight because being gay was so hard and dangerous in the world. The thing is, being gay is even easier than being black or a woman, and much easier than being gay and pretending and forcing myself to be straight.—X, discussing her coming-out experience

X is a Black cisgender woman who identifies as a lesbian. She was born in 1998 and grew up lower middle class in a suburban neighborhood in Texas.

Sex education was minimal; X only learned about the physical parts of the reproductive system, pregnancy, and sexually transmitted infections, in an abstinence-only curriculum. There was no information about sexual orientation or emotional aspects of dating. Puberty was unpleasant and peers were generally unsupportive. X's mother was supportive but very much wanted her to choose the "best" option at all times.

In high school, she learned a lot more about sex education, sexuality, and safety from Tumblr blogs. One blog in particular, a sapphic[6] sexual education blog, helped her figure out her sexuality at age sixteen. She started to wonder about her sexual feelings when she was playing a video game that had a female character cross-dressing and passing as a male pirate captain. She loved the character and was shaken up when it was revealed she was actually a woman. She started questioning her sexuality, and Tumblr and Reddit[7] came to the rescue with resources and Q&As. Years of seeing positive representation of queer people made it easier to accept herself.

Initially, X only came out to close friends who had already come out to her as gay or bisexual. She knew that they would be supportive. She chose to remain closeted to straight friends until she had a girlfriend in college; she didn't want them to feel uncomfortable and think she might be attracted to them. Since then, she has come out to select people she trusts: "Not everyone deserves to know about my life and I like to keep it that way."

To make adolescence easier for queer youth, X thinks that there should be queer representation in the school curriculum and acknowledgement that not all youth are straight. She also thinks it would be helpful to have a "beginner's guide" to realizing that you're gay, with affirming questions and answers.

DEMOGRAPHICS

In this section, we are introduced to the demographics of the participants as a whole. Participants shared about their gender identities, trans status, gender pronouns, sexual orientations, intersex status, ethnicities, the years in which they were born, the states where they grew up, the kinds of neighborhoods they grew up in, and their socioeconomic classes growing up. Not all participants chose to fill out the demographics section of the survey, and others filled out some but not all of the questions. Furthermore, many participants selected more than one option for demographic elements like gender identity, where they may identify as more than one gender or use more than one term for their gender, or location, if they grew up in more than one state. This means the data doesn't always add up to 150 participants.

Gender Identity

Possible responses on the survey were woman, man, nonbinary, agender, Two-Spirit, and other (write in). The majority of participants were women (54), followed by men (32) and nonbinary people (31). Six participants were agender and two were Two-Spirit. Two participants were in the process of questioning their gender identities and wrote in "Questioning" and "???," while eleven others ticked the "other" box and wrote in more granular gender identities under the nonbinary umbrella. "Other" responses included girlflux[8] (1), demigirl[9] (2), Autigender (1), demiagender[10] (1), fa'atane[11] (1), multigender[12] (1), genderqueer (2), neutrois (1), and genderfluid[13] (1).

Trans Status

Fifty-one participants identified as transgender and/or nonbinary, while sixty-seven identified as cisgender or non-transgender. One participant wrote in fa'atane and another wrote that they were questioning whether they were transgender.

Pronouns

Gender pronouns were a write-in question and answers matched nearly evenly with the expected gender identities: Sixty-three people used she/her/hers, forty-one people used he/him/his, and forty people used they/them/theirs. While in the 1990s and 2000s there seemed to be many nonbinary folks using neopronouns such as ze/hir/hirs, the current trend seems to be singular they. One participant had no preference, two were currently considering neopronouns and several wrote in more than one pronoun.

Sexual Orientation

Possible responses on the survey were lesbian, gay, bisexual, queer, asexual, pansexual, and other with a write-in option. The majority of participants were bisexual (39), followed by queer (32) and asexual (28). Considering the popularly cited research that posits that asexuals make up about 1 percent of the population,[14] the number in this sample is quite high. I did target the less visible populations, including asexuals, in my recruiting efforts, and can only assume that asexuals are especially generous with research participation.

Other participants identified as pansexual (23), lesbian (21), and gay (12). Twelve ticked the "other" box and wrote in other identities. One of these was straight. This was a major oversight on my part; this should have been included in the list of possible answers, as many transgender people identify as straight or heterosexual. "Other" answers included straight (4), demisexual (4), biromantic (2), demipansexual[15] (1), and gray-aromantic[16] (1).

Intersex Status

One hundred eight participants were certain that they were not intersex, two were unsure, and seven participants were intersex. This number is a bit higher than expected,[17] perhaps due to recruitment in intersex communities online. Additionally, some people go through their lives without knowing that they are intersex; some variations are discerned only after fertility issues are explored.

Ethnicity

The ethnicity section was write-in to allow for more granular and multifaceted responses. The vast majority of respondents were white (101) and non-Hispanic/Latinx[18] (116). This was probably because I was unable to recruit in BIPOC (Black, Indigenous, and People of Color) spaces due to being declined or ignored by moderators, as well as time constraints. Nonwhite participants included Asian Americans (7), Native Americans/Alaska Natives (5), Black Americans. (5), and Native Hawaiians/Pacific Islanders (2). Five people identified themselves as Hispanic/Latinx.

Year Born

Participants skewed very young, with the majority (48 people) born between the years 1996 and 2000. The next biggest cohort (27 people) was born between 1991 and 1995; the one after that (18 people) born between 1986 and 1990; and the one after that (12 people) born between 1981 and 1985. A small handful of participants was born between 1951 and 1980. This positions the majority of participants as Millennials/Generation Y and Generation Z. This is fitting since the subject of queer adolescence is a current one, so the collected recommendations for support are timely.

Location

Participants were very evenly distributed across forty-two states in all quadrants, with some bunches occurring in California and Washington state. This is likely due to snowball sampling from my original post on my personal Facebook page; I live in California and have friends in Washington. Some participants lived in one state their entire adolescence, while others moved around.

Neighborhood

A majority of participants (77) grew up in suburban neighborhoods. Thirty-eight grew up rural and twenty grew up urban. Four participants wrote in that they lived on military bases growing up. Many participants moved between neighborhood types.

Class

Socioeconomic class was defined as follows: Upper class—highly affluent; upper middle class—educated professionals; middle class—white-collar professionals; lower middle class—semi-professional with some college education; working class—clerical and blue collar; and lower class—working poor and unemployed. Most participants (40) grew up upper middle class. Only two participants grew up upper class and twelve grew up lower class. The rest were fairly evenly distributed into middle class (30), lower middle class (27), and working class (29). I can only guess why most participants grew up upper middle class—perhaps because this demographic tends to be very computer savvy and often has the privilege to be more open about their gender and/or sexual orientation minority status.

3

SEX EDUCATION

Sexuality and reproductive health education is vital to help youth learn about their bodies, sex and reproduction, gender and sexuality, and healthy relationships. This chapter explores how participants learned sex education, what they learned (and what was left out), and the quality of teaching and learning.

Sex education quality and content varies widely from state to state. Only twenty-four states and Washington, DC, currently require public schools to teach sex education, and of these only thirteen require the sex education to be medically accurate.[1] Many school programs are abstinence-only by law, due either to ideology or to acceptance of federal grant moneys for abstinence-only education.[2] In states that mandate an abstinence-only curriculum, rates of chlamydia and gonorrhea are higher than in states that cover STI prevention such as barrier methods. Likewise, in states that mandate an abstinence-only curriculum, rates of teen pregnancy and birth are significantly higher than in states that discuss pregnancy prevention.[3]

Even in public schools that include education on pregnancy and STI prevention, most stop there and avoid topics of consent and healthy relationships. Moreover, very few schools have queer-inclusive sex education curricula. As of August 2019, only five states mandate LGBTQIA+-inclusive curricula: California, New Jersey, Colorado, Oregon, and Illinois.[4] Even so, the inclusive curricula laws don't specify queer inclusion in sex education units.

Some students receive sex education through church programming, either as a supplement to or instead of school-based learning. Faith-based sex education varies as well. Programs like True Love Waits, for example, are abstinence-only and involve public vows of chastity. On the other hand, programs like Our Whole Lives are comprehensive and include discussion of sexual ethics and decision making, as well as queer content.[5]

HOW WE LEARNED

Many participants received formal sex education, either through school or church programming. Some also learned through parents, caregivers, friends, and peers. Most supplemented what they learned from others with personal research via books and the internet.

Formal Programming

Eighty-seven participants indicated that they had received formal sex education through school, and five received sex education through church programming. Several participants' parents signed a form to prevent them from attending sex education classes on religious grounds. Some participants' schools didn't offer sex education classes at all.

These experiences match the data from the 2017 GLSEN National School Survey, which surveyed the school experiences of LGBTQ youth in kindergarten through twelfth grade. Over one-fifth of LGBTQIA+ students in the survey had not received any sex education at all; not all states mandate sex education, and parents do have the option to opt out of the curriculum.[6]

School sex education curricula varied by comprehensiveness and quality. Most participants learned about anatomy and hygiene; many learned about heterosexual sex and reproduction; and very few learned about gender, sexual orientation, or healthy relationships. This topic is discussed further in the "What We Learned" section.

Some church-based sex education was comprehensive, while others were unhelpful and conservative. QA's experience was a common one: "My sex education came through a course called 'Created by God' through our church. It discussed the mechanics of sex between a heterosexual couple and some general hygiene and nothing more."

Parents and Caregivers

Thirty-eight participants received some form of sex education from their parents or caregivers. Often this came in the form of mothers educating daughters (and transmasculine children) about the signs of getting a period and how to manage it. Parents and caregivers also provided education in the form of gender and sexuality policing; puberty often came with new rules about clothing, grooming, and opposite-gender friendships.

Some parents were able to provide a more comprehensive and age-appropriate sex education to their children. EAA recalls, "We had ducks, and I remember being five or six, and asking my mom why Mama Duck was giving Buddy a piggyback ride. She used that time to explain sex to me in an age-appropriate way." Other parents were less confident with these topics and refused to discuss them or provided limited details. Peri says, "My parents were willing to speak about [sex] in the most PG terms, but unless I brought the conversation to the table, they sort of glossed over that part of life."

Friends and Peers

Friends and peers were sources of sexual information as well. Sometimes this information was useful and factual. Ellie, for example, learned a lot from a young friend: "[She] was a biology student and fascinated with the human body and taught me much of the sex ed I didn't get at home." Other times, information from friends was extraordinarily unhelpful. Kate learned some interesting details from a friend in elementary school: "For a long time, I thought that sperm was like a freaky snake tongue that would get ejected out of the penis during sex and then get sucked back in, that condoms were literally plastic shopping bags, and that the hymen grows back every time."

Peers and society at large often provided direction in the form of gender and sexual policing. Participants whose bodies transgressed social norms were often called out and picked on. Many female participants were bullied, stared at, and made fun of for having leg or armpit hair. Often, this resulted in them shaving despite not wishing to. Many male participants were equally policed for being chubby or having more breast tissue than was judged "normal." This form of education taught participants to change their bodies, present differently, or hide.

Personal Research

Most participants supplemented what they learned from formal programming and informal conversations with personal research. LAA remembers, "I educated myself on the internet from age twelve on about less 'sterile' aspects of sex and sexuality, primarily by reading message boards and erotica and then looking up medical resources based on what I found informally." For CA, "The schools I attended were conservative, so they refrained from teaching much sex ed. I decided to educate myself using biology/anatomy books and the internet toward the end of high school."

Some participants used books, such as romance novels, sexual health texts, and anatomical reference books. Unfortunately, romance novels and other erotica are often poor representations of sex and sexuality, with inaccurate anatomy, unlikely sexual positions, and often lack of explicit consent. Sexual health texts are generally better in terms of factual information, but often lack LGBTQIA+ representation, contain biological essentialism such as saying that all girls have vaginas, and have heteronormative assumptions such as assuming that everybody will end up in a heterosexual marriage and will procreate. Anatomical reference books are useful but generally lack information about the mechanics of sex.

Most participants used the internet as their primary source of personal research on sex education topics. Some did research on factual sites such as Planned Parenthood, Scarleteen, and the Centers for Disease Control and Prevention, but most gravitated to message boards, chat rooms, erotica, and personal blogs. These informal sites can be a wonderful way for people to connect and share personal anecdotes, but they can also be rife with misinformation. Erotica and pornography, for example, can certainly teach some of the mechanics of sex but generally lack discussion of safer sex, consent, and healthy relationships.

Still, even if some of the information learned through personal research may be flawed or incomplete, it is empowering for young people to seek out their own information and their own representation to make up for a poor formal sex education curriculum. Self-education can be a form of everyday resistance: Young LGBTQIA+ people are marginalized both in terms of age and gender/sexuality, and rebelling against the paucity of information provided to them in school by locating useful and relevant resources on their own is a powerful form of resistance and empowerment.[7]

WHAT WE LEARNED

LGBTQIA+ youth have considerable health disparities as compared to their cisgender and heterosexual counterparts. For example, young gay and bisexual men are at increased risk of HIV, syphilis, and other sexually transmitted infections (STIs), while young lesbian and bisexual women experience pregnancy at higher rates than their heterosexual peers. Additionally, LGBTQIA+ youth experience significantly higher levels of physical and sexual violence and bullying and are at higher risk of suicidal ideation and suicide attempts.[8]

Inclusive and comprehensive sexuality education results in better health outcomes for queer students. Unfortunately, the majority of sex education programs are exclusionary. Some states even prohibit positive representation of homosexuality under "no promo homo" laws.[9] In these states, queer youth experience a more hostile school climate, have less access to queer-inclusive curricular resources, are less likely to feel supported by educators, and have less access to relevant health resources.[10]

Most participants in this study received some form of sexuality education, but very few received comprehensive and queer-inclusive sex education. Most learned about anatomy, hygiene, heterosexual sex, and reproduction. A much smaller number learned about gender, sexual orientation, and healthy relationships.

Anatomy and Hygiene

Fifty-three participants learned about human sexual anatomy, though many were limited to learning only about their own sexual parts. Many school programs separated the classes into boys and girls to teach about body parts and either menstrual management or nocturnal emissions. Maddie's experience was that "sex ed at my school pretty much only taught us how to use deodorant and that girls get periods."

Rose had a slightly more thorough education: "When I was ten, my elementary school separated girls and boys and showed us a film about puberty, menstruation, and reproduction. It was helpful and informative, but it was very awkward to be split up from the boys, and I never understood why we had to be in separate rooms to learn about our bodies. It made me feel that menstruation and sexuality were shameful, secret things."

A few participants did not even receive anatomy instruction. Joe's experience was that "the class never even covered basic human anatomy. I didn't learn that there was a difference between the vagina and urethra until I was eighteen when I bought my first box of tampons and read the instructions provided inside." This particular experience—learning vulvar anatomy from a tampon box—was mentioned by several participants.

Others received anatomy and hygiene education that was so vague and euphemistic they did not understand it. Seren, for example, watched a video about "wetting the bed" that she didn't realize was about nocturnal emissions, even when she had experienced them first-hand.

Sex and Reproduction

Thirty-eight participants learned about sex and reproduction in their sexuality education programs. Most participants learned about sexually transmitted infections, but this information was imparted in a highly stigmatized way. Many people recalled slide shows showing late-stage infection in the genitals that were obviously shared in order to frighten youth into avoiding sexual contact.

FA shares, "In school we were mostly taught about abstinence, and photos of STIs were used as a scare tactic to steer us away from having sex before marriage." DA's experience was similar: "My school used an abstinence-only program, so I didn't really learn much about the actual act of sex. Instead, I mostly learned about STIs and the 'horrors' of premarital sex. Everything that I learned was in the context of hetero-sexual relationships."

Gender and Sexual Orientation

Only three participants received information about gender and sexual orientation in their sexuality education classes. For example, participant I recalls that "the comprehensive sex ed I received acknowledged and spoke to the experiences of queer and trans folks in a non-stigmatizing way."

Most participants instead received negative messages about LGBTQIA+ topics from peers, family, and the wider society. In Joe's experience, "My little knowledge of sexuality came in the form of what I could see and hear, which was that heterosexuality is the default and anything other than that was bad. My peers used the term 'gay' as an insult, and the first openly gay student I met in high school was bullied and ostracized by most of the school."

Similarly, Rose recalls, "I learned from watching my parents' reactions to Ellen DeGeneres and Rosie O'Donnell that being gay or lesbian (the only non-heterosexual orientations I knew at the time) was not a 'good' thing to be." L. Poe "learned about trans people from bad TLC documentaries and Jerry Springer."

On the other hand, some participants received positive messages about queer people outside of formal programming. For Zoe, "I grew up in a part of Washington that had good support and communities for people in this group, which really helped expose me to LGBTQIA culture from a young age. My first time understanding what gay meant was attending a gay/lesbian wedding with my sister and mom."

Healthy Relationships

Only one participant learned anything about healthy relationships from school sex education. RK's sex education included "anatomy, STIs, and pregnancy in depth, and some more relationship-oriented and emotional aspects of sexuality. The ability for men to also be raped was brought up, so we must have been very progressive for the time." RK was lucky. The majority of sex education programming doesn't include the topic of healthy relationships at all. Many participants lamented the absence of the topics of consent and dating violence.

QUALITY OF TEACHING AND LEARNING

As we have already seen, the quality of teaching varies considerably. Participants discussed abstinence-only curricula, heteronormativity, levels of comprehension, and queer inclusion.

Abstinence-Only

Thirty-five participants mentioned that their sex education programming was abstinence based. This means that while pregnancy and STIs may be discussed, birth control such as condoms are left out entirely because students are expected and encouraged to abstain from having premarital sex. In G's experience, "The religion classes taught that sex was evil and you would get an STD and get pregnant, unless it was done in marriage, where women had to defer to their husbands' sexual appetite and not have any of their own."

Similarly, X says, "We only learned about the physical parts of the reproductive system and what happens when you screw up (you get STDs and pregnant). The best way to avoid this is to be abstinent. Nothing about sexuality and nothing about dating." When students do not receive information about safer sex practices, they don't have lower rates of premarital sex; instead, they have higher rates of pregnancy and STIs because they don't know how to protect themselves.

Heteronormative

Fifty-eight participants learned sexuality education in a heteronormative context. This means that students were assumed to be heterosexual, sex was expected to be procreative, and people were expected to progress from heterosexual dating to marriage to reproduction. Skylar, for example, "grew up in an evangelical church, so the only option was heterosexuality (and cisgender)." Fellow participant 'Uhane "learned nothing about gender, sexual orientation, or even my own medical (intersex) condition until I was in college and making my own decisions."

Sometimes, queerness is brought up in a heteronormative context, but only in a negative way, to dismiss or discourage it. In NAA's sex education curriculum, "There was no mention of trans people. Gay and lesbian people were only brought up in the context of HIV. I learned about sex pretty much exclusively from my peers and online porn."

Other participants did learn about safer sex, but only in a heteronormative context. GA says, "I was lucky enough to learn about safe sex instead of just abstinence, but we didn't talk about sexuality or gender at school."

Sparse/Basic

Nineteen participants complained that their sexuality education was sparse or basic. Another fifteen said that their education was outdated and religious. We've already learned that many participants did not receive complete information about their sexual anatomy or received only vague or euphemistic information about hygiene topics. Four participants specifically mentioned that there was no mention of intersex conditions in their sex education, but zero participants mentioned learning about intersex conditions, so I think it's safe to assume that intersex conditions were rarely if ever discussed in the sex education programming experienced by the participants in this study.

Several participants mentioned that they received only very basic scientific information. For WA, "My sex education was absolutely unacceptable. It was watching a video from the '80s about genitalia and talk about STDs in the ninth grade. I learned 90 percent of what I know from the internet." A common theme is that participants learned more from self-study than from formal programming; A recalls, "I learned most everything I know about these subjects from my peers, cheesy romance novels, online, and my boyfriend at the time."

Comprehensive

Only nine participants reported that they had received comprehensive sexuality education. The American College of Obstetricians and Gynecologists (ACOG) says that comprehensive sexuality education should be being medically accurate and evidence based; should provide information about pregnancy and STI prevention; and should also teach about "forms of sexual expression, healthy sexual and nonsexual relationships, gender identity and sexual orientation and questioning, communication, recognizing and preventing sexual violence, consent, and decision making."[11] Lofty goals, indeed. I suspect most of the participants stating that their sex education was comprehensive were actually merely indicating that their programs were not abstinence based.

Inclusive

Only three participants received queer-inclusive sexuality education. Even then, some inclusive programming left out important details. In Aly's experience, "Both my school class and books included basic information about orientations, but neither included information about asexuality." Other times, teachers attempted to be inclusive but missed the mark. Nora remembers, "The only time I ever heard non-cis straight people referenced was when we discussed dental dams, and even then the teacher said it and the class made jokes and the teacher simply moved along."

These participants' experiences show that sexuality education is incredibly varied in the United States. While many students receive sex education in school, that education may be abstinence-only, use STI images as scare tactics, contain only basic information or false information, and leave out LGBTQIA+ experiences entirely or mention them only in terms of HIV exposure. On the other hand, education could include queer representation, information about consent and healthy relationships, and age-appropriate details about the mechanics of sex as well as sexual ethics. Unfortunately, most of these participants' experiences fall into the former category.

4

GOING THROUGH PUBERTY

In this chapter, we discuss what the experience of puberty was like for our participants. Puberty, as a developmental milestone, has many dimensions; participants focused on psychological and experiential aspects. Many participants also talked about what they learned during puberty separate from formal sexuality and reproductive health education.

PSYCHOLOGICAL ASPECTS OF PUBERTY

Puberty was psychologically challenging for many participants. Several participants reported experiencing gender dysphoria during puberty. A few participants were victims of traumatic events. Many developed depression and anxiety. Several reported feeling different, especially feeling ugly, in relation to their peers. Some felt they had an unremarkable or typical puberty. And some acquired early queer self-knowledge.

Dysphoria

Twenty-six participants experienced intense gender dysphoria during puberty. Those assigned female at birth articulated their discomfort with breast development and menstruation; those assigned male at birth discussed feeling uncomfortable with facial and body hair as well as genital growth and nocturnal emissions.

Primary and secondary sexual characteristics change and develop a lot during puberty. Prepubertal bodies are somewhat similar in terms of generally flat chests and small genitalia. Many participants mentioned feeling comfortable in their prepubertal bodies but suddenly developing dysphoria due to the changes occurring in their bodies upon puberty.

Lane, for example, "hated my female body . . . I didn't want those bumps on me. I wanted my flat chest back. To be able to run around the house shirtless, free." Cecily's experience was similar: "I didn't want to wear a bra. I just didn't even want to acknowledge that I had breasts because I was horrified that they were there." Although many adolescents might miss the freedom of childhood nudity and being basically sexless, the type of discomfort Lane and Cecily articulate is more extreme, intensely felt, and psychologically serious. Dysphoria can take up someone's day-to-day life with perseverating thoughts, anxiety, and self-loathing.

Seren experienced dysphoria with her newly growing facial hair:

> As my facial hair came in more, I felt more and more horrible. I didn't understand why, but I really didn't like my face in pictures. It always looked like I had weird shadows on my face. I thought I was ugly and I only looked good in certain lighting. It turned out the lighting was yellow light, where my facial hair didn't show up in the photos much or at all. The shadows weren't coming from the light, they were living right underneath my skin.

Seren's dysphoria continued through adolescence into adulthood. She didn't pinpoint that it was gender dysphoria until she had the words to articulate her gendered self as an adult. She just thought that she was ugly and often refused to allow photographs to be taken of her.

Other participants mentioned testicular and penis growth as being their main dysphoria concern. Others talked about menarche and menstruation. Joe, for example, experienced "a mixture of shame and emotional discomfort when I would have my periods, which, retrospectively, was due to a mixture of societal silence around menstruation and minor dysphoria." When LA got their first period, "I was so angry. I remember asking my mom why she didn't get the doctors to remove my uterus when I was a baby. She didn't know how to respond to that." Any characteristic or process that sets a person apart as a (wrongly) gendered subject is a possible focus for dysphoria.

Trauma

Thirteen participants described puberty as being traumatic. This is sadly common; lesbian, gay, bisexual, transgender, and queer youth experience trauma at higher rates than their cisheterosexual peers.[1] LGBTQIA+ youth experience higher rates of physical violence, sexual violence, electronic and face-to-face bullying, threats or violence with weapons, and dating violence.

Study participants talked about living through sexual or physical abuse, neglect, sexual harassment, or bullying at school. For GA, "puberty was awful. I was bullied, isolated, and alone." Other participants described childhood sexual abuse as complicating their pubertal debuts. They unfortunately already knew what sex was and were distressed at developing secondary sexual characteristics because it might bring on more abuse. Other participants experienced an uptick in physical abuse from parents or other adults in their life corresponding with pubertal changes. And some participants were neglected by the adults in their lives and had to fend for themselves when it came to researching and purchasing hygiene supplies such as menstrual pads and deodorant.

Depression and Anxiety

Many participants described emotional turmoil during puberty that could be described as depression and/or anxiety. LGBTQIA+ youth are at higher risk for depression, suicide, substance use, and other psychological disorders than their cisheterosexual peers.[2] Nine participants specifically mentioned suicidal ideation or attempts, and one mentioned having an eating disorder during puberty. GA, for example, "tried to kill myself four times when I was fifteen. I spent my adolescence terrified of being gay and pretending I wasn't. Even when I was willing to admit I was into girls I still only dated men. I tried to choose to be straight." GA's suicidality was connected directly to shame about her sexual orientation. W, too, connected suicidality with queer feelings: "I hated my body and was ashamed of my feelings. I thought about killing myself a lot."

Some participants were lied to about having intersex[3] conditions. Learning about their conditions later in life caused them significant distress. 'Uhane, for example, "learned the facts of my intersex issue in my middle twenties. The facts of it were more devastating than they were empowering. Honestly, I wonder why I didn't jump in front of a train that day."

One participant mentioned developing an eating disorder in adolescence. Gay, lesbian, and bisexual youth are at higher risk of developing eating disorders than their heterosexual counterparts.[4] Disordered eating in this population (like others) is about control over the body and often a sense of personal unattractiveness or hatred of the body. Participant I said, "I had disordered eating habits during puberty which I now see as connected to feelings and emotions within my experience of gender and sexuality." There may have been others with similar experiences, but none shared them.

Feeling Different

Many participants reported feeling different from their peers. Five used the term "different" and seven used the term "ugly" to describe their assessment of themselves during puberty. Sometimes this feeling was connected with gender or sexual identity. Maddie, for example, says, "I started feeling really ugly all the time during puberty. I felt especially ugly when I realized that I was having romantic/sexual thoughts about other girls my age. I assumed that all lesbians were ugly, masculine, dumb, fat, loud, and annoying." In this case, stereotypical representations of queer people made Maddie terrified that she would fit the stereotype and resulted in an intense self-loathing.

Some asexual participants noted that lacking the sexual drive for peers made them feel different. CA remembers, "It was strange. I constantly thought I should be doing things/dating, but I never found anyone attractive. I thought I was broken for a long time." In puberty, differences are magnified, and peers notice them and often point them out, so any little deviation from the "norm" (whatever that is) is often perceived as horribly different and uncomfortable.

Unremarkable

Despite the many recollections of unpleasant or difficult experiences during puberty, twenty-four participants had a completely unremarkable pubertal experience. RK thinks "it was surprisingly typical[.] I remember being so proud of my nice arm peach fuzz. People also got really curious in the locker room, and the extra muscle development was nice." Seemingly normative development in step with peers offered a sense of safety and security to many folks.

Others didn't remember much about puberty because it felt so ordinary. O, for example, recalls that "I didn't really notice any changes until after they were complete." S says, "Puberty was nothing notable, everything happened like my parents said it would." WA had a sense of humor about their experience: "Puberty was not too bad. They said you'll get hairy, smelly, and gross and I sure did." For Q, "I don't remember anything remarkable about puberty except that it took me several years to figure out how to properly use a tampon." This last experience was fairly common; the learning curve for locating the vagina seems to be somewhat steep for some folks.

Some participants had received such shoddy sex education that they didn't understand they were going through puberty at the time. For Erin, "I didn't learn any sex education through my parents and school really. The only thing I remember was getting acne. I would get erections and I didn't know what they meant."

Early Queer Self-Knowledge

Quite a few participants—twenty-eight—reported realizing their gender or sexual identities during puberty or earlier. Of these, five remained closeted through adolescence. For some participants, this early queer self-knowledge was devastating. For Peri, "when the hormones hit, I was a wreck. Especially when I found out I was attracted to both sexes and the feeling wasn't fading. I was taught that it was a common phase that people grow out of. I wasn't growing out of it and I was terrified."

FAA remembers, "I was getting severely depressed due to dysphoria, but nobody would tell me what I was feeling or tell me that I'm not supposed to be feeling that way. It was also about the same time I realized I was attracted to girls and the religious influences in my life felt the need to make me feel guilty and disgusted with myself."

Others connected their gender or sexual identity to puberty seeming late or early. Rose recalls, "I read the Bible often growing up, and I was always afraid of being 'barren,' which I thought meant that your menarche never arrived . . . . [A]t one point, I thought that maybe God was punishing me for my feelings toward girls by delaying my menarche." Other participants with religious backgrounds also felt ashamed of their early queer feelings. EAA "started noticing girls around that time, and trying to ignore that I noticed girls and tried to pray the queer away."

EXPERIENTIAL ASPECTS OF PUBERTY

In terms of experiential aspects of puberty, some participants had troublesome experiences while others grew and developed with relative ease. Of the difficulties, participants mentioned developing earlier, later, or differently than their peers. Some also discussed specific hygiene challenges. Many AFAB[5] participants had menstrual discomfort and difficulties. Others experienced sexual harassment or bullying at school. And some participants reported early sexual experimentation.

Developmental Timeline

While most participants felt that they developed apace with their peers, five felt that they developed late, ten felt that they developed early, and two intersex participants felt that they developed differently than their peers.

Later developers felt an intense sense of embarrassment at being "late bloomers." During puberty, youth tend to hyper-fixate on their development in relation to their peers. Still being flat-chested or beardless when all one's peers have developed these secondary sex characteristics can make one feel immature and can open someone up to being made fun of or even bullied, especially in spaces like locker rooms where these developmental lags are easier to notice.

Similarly, earlier development could invoke a sense of embarrassment because of the scrutiny the participant receives from peers. Especially for participants assigned female at birth, early breast development can cause deep feelings of shame around being stared at. As well, some participants felt panicky at not being able to be children anymore. Lane recalls, "I was not informed that you could hit puberty at a young age. I hit it at age nine. I developed breasts and I cried my eyes out." Likewise, EA says that "puberty was horrible in the beginning because I was so young. In sex ed when the teacher was talking about breasts, I crossed my arms over my chest because I was the only one with breasts."

Some intersex participants remember their pubertal development being distinctly different than their peers'. Intersex means sexual or reproductive anatomy that doesn't fit the typical definitions of male or female. Physical sex is located in the chromosomes, sex hormones, gonads, genitals, and secondary sex characteristics. For some people—as many as one in one hundred—one or more of these are atypical. Some babies are born with "ambiguous genitalia" which often results in nonconsensual genital surgery. Other people don't realize they have an intersex condition until puberty, or until they have fertility issues as an adult, or never at all.[6]

Tommie Jayne, for example, "was lied to about the genital surgery when I was a child and didn't really learn that I have an intersex condition until I came out in about 2010." 'Uhane remembers, "I didn't get anywhere near the same experience in puberty that all of my guy friends seemed to get. They'd talk about things as though the experiences were shouting in their ears while all I heard were faint whispers." PA noticed signs of their intersex condition as an adolescent, but the facts were concealed by their parents and doctors. "There were signs during puberty with feminine hips in the boys' locker room. After I had my vaginoplasty, my surgeon noted that there was scar tissue in my genital area indicating that some sort of surgery was performed there when I was born confirming what I had expected my entire life."

Hygiene Hassles

Five participants discussed feeling embarrassed and exasperated with hygiene issues during puberty. Common targets for frustration were body odor and deodorant, facial and body hair and shaving, and menstruation and menstrual hygiene products. For some participants, body odor was experienced as so extreme that deodorant didn't work—or bothered sensitive skin. Shaving caused breakouts and ingrown hairs for some participants. And several mentioned hating using menstrual products due to discomfort, hatred of menstruation, or user difficulty with inserting tampons or changing pads in a timely enough manner.

Menstrual Difficulties

Three participants mentioned having very difficult menstrual periods. Participant A recalls, "Puberty was annoying. My menstrual cycle was incredibly painful, I started getting unwanted attention from adult men, and just a general discomfort in being in my body." Similarly, P remembers, "My periods were excruciatingly painful and heavy. I always felt like my body was wrong." For some participants, menstrual pain was dismissed by parents and doctors, even though the cause was later revealed to be endometriosis or uterine fibroids. This disheartening experience may be due to disbelief of women's pain and other self-reported symptoms.

Two additional participants weren't certain about their first menstrual period. One participant thought their first menarche was feces, because they didn't have the full facts on how menstrual fluid looks different from regular blood. PAA reveals that "despite being educated on what periods were, I was still really confused when I first got mine. When it first showed up, it was brown, so you can imagine what I thought. I just thought something was wrong with me and was silently freaking out." Another participant, Kae, wasn't fully educated on periods and thought they had a genital injury: "I remember when I got my first period, because I didn't know what was happening to me and thought I had injured myself somehow."

Sexual Harassment and Bullying

A truly discouraging number of participants—sixteen—reported experiencing sexual harassment and bullying during puberty. Sexual harassment came from peers, family members, and adult male strangers. Bullying was school based and perpetrated by peers. Harassment and bullying caused many participants to hate and fear their own bodies. OA recalls, "I started experiencing street harassment or inappropriate attention from adult cis men around age ten." Similarly, Nora says, "I have resented my breasts ever since the first time an adult man came on to me in public—I was eleven."

Early Sexual Experimentation

Four participants reported early sexual experimentation (prior to high school) with same-sex partners. Same-sex sexual play is normal in pre-adolescence.[7] What's interesting is that these participants were acting on genuine same-sex desire rather than simple curiosity. They were the same participants that articulated very early queer self-knowledge.

FURTHER EDUCATION

Some participants reported being surprised by some physiological aspects of puberty and reflected that they wished they had learned more in sex education curricula. Others received information during puberty that was medically inaccurate. Tampons were a source of (mis)information for several participants. Finally, many participants felt pushed toward compulsory girl- or boyhood by parents, peers, and the wider society.

That Wasn't in Sex Ed

Quite a few participants—twenty-three—had to quickly learn about pubertal milestones by direct experience, as they had missed vital information from sex education. Some common experiences included confusion about menarche and menstruation, surprise at first ejaculation, and being lied to about intersex conditions. For HAA,

> Puberty was concerning and unsettling because no one really warned me about the changes to my body and behavior that would happen. I didn't understand what erections were or that they were even tied to sex for a long time. Wet dreams distressed me so much that I would wake up and hurt myself trying to stop them. I thought even involuntary moments of sexuality like that might doom me to hell, especially because of the content of the dreams.

Christina was also shocked by her first ejaculation: "When I first started masturbating, I had no idea what orgasm was. When I had my first orgasm, I thought I was having an emergency of some sort, it totally surprised me."

Inaccurate Medical Information

Four participants received inaccurate medical information, including pregnancy prevention tips such as douching or having sex while menstruating. Another common inaccuracy was that periods were supposed to be excruciatingly painful (so endometriosis and fibroids went undetected for years), that participants were dyadic (intersexuality was concealed), and virginity myths such as the supposed inability to use tampons in a virginal state.

Tampons

There were many mentions of lessons about or from tampons. Four participants specifically mentioned learning vulvar anatomy from the informational insert found in tampon boxes. Before that, they mistook the urethra for the vagina or thought that the urethra was in the clitoris. And one participant recalled being told that tampons would "take" one's virginity. Nora recalls, "I started buying and wearing tampons on my own around fourteen, and when my dad found them he became enraged—he truly believed you had to have 'lost your virginity' to be able to use tampons."

Compulsory Girlhood/Boyhood

Compulsory girlhood/womanhood and boyhood/manhood was another common theme. Upon reaching puberty, participants were expected to behave and appear as the gender matching their sex assigned at birth. Furthermore, they were expected to follow the cisheteronormative trajectory of opposite-sex dating, marriage, and reproduction. Although many parents were supportive once their children came out, the ingrained expectation was still painful and challenging for the youth.

Perhaps the most vivid way compulsory girlhood was enforced was during the milestone of the first menstruation. Several participants were told "you're a woman now" upon reaching menarche. Nora's experience was especially cringeworthy: "My mother started yelling and crying and shouting that I was a woman now in the middle of the public camp shower. My dad bought me pads the size of Texas and insisted on walking into the campsite holding them up." For some participants, menarche was something to be celebrated, but for many others, they preferred it to be a private affair that they may or may not be excited about. Certainly, being told that one is a "woman now" can be disconcerting to a relative child, particularly if that child doesn't actually identify as a girl or woman.

Advertisements for hygiene items often clearly position the item not only as heavily gendered, but also necessary for the purchaser to fulfil their ideal masculinity or femininity. For example, men's deodorant advertisements often feature an exceptionally masculine man—tall, muscular, bearded, and often white—participating in sports or outdoors adventures. Similarly, advertisements for menstrual hygiene items often feature women who are the epitome of femininity in our society—thin, beautiful, and generally white—showing off their ability to participate in feminine activities, such as walking on the beach wearing white clothing, despite menstruating. Advertisements like these push ideas of compulsory boyhood and girlhood to adolescents as well as adults. They can be especially damaging to youth who are questioning their sexuality or gender identity.

5

PARENTAL AND PEER INVOLVEMENT

The people in LGBTQIA+ youths' lives have a significant impact on their development and wellness, including during adolescence. This chapter explores how family members, friends and peers, teachers and other school staff, queer-specific programming, and the wider society interact with queer youth, with either support, negligence, or cruelty.

SUPPORTIVE COMMUNITY MEMBERS

Many study participants had wonderfully supportive families, great friend groups, and fantastic teachers who all supported them through adolescence, discovering their identities, and coming out. Often this entailed explicit support such as puberty education, revealing their queer-supportive values, and assisting youth in accessing resources and further support. Just as often, it entailed implicit displays of support such as good boundaries, trust, and honest communication. These youth tended to report an easier adolescence, less confusion about identity, and earlier coming out.

Family Members

Thirty-two participants reported having supportive families. Much support came through novel hygiene instruction. Many AFAB participants learned about how to use a menstrual pad or shave their legs from their mothers or sisters. Many AMAB participants learned about how to shave their faces and use deodorant from their fathers or other male family members. Lane, for example, remembers, "My stepmom told me about periods and the signs of getting them. My stepsister taught me how to shave my legs." Maddie had a similar experience: "My mom was very positive, and taught us about hormone fluctuations, that it's normal to have wild mood swings, basic menstrual hygiene, etc." Kae says, "My mom was very supportive. She went about it in a 'this is just a thing that happens' way, which I appreciated."

Some mothers were very hands-on about menstrual hygiene instruction. These mothers showed children how to adhere a pad to their underwear, went over the tampon instructions with them, and showed them how to manage and avoid bloodstains. EAA remembers, "My mom bought me pads, and showed me how to rinse my underwear out in cold water." A few participants received a menarche gift; for BA, "My mom gave me a ring that her aunt had given her for my first period."

For K, "My mother was probably my biggest source of support during puberty. She taught me about menstrual hygiene, bought me skin products for my acne, and just reassured me that everything was going to be OK. If I didn't have her support, I don't know what I would've done." HAA recalls, "My parents were supportive about the body changes, reassuring me that they were normal and helping my self-esteem during this time." Peri says, "My family was supportive in the ways they knew how to be. The physical changes they warned me about and helped me address." And for AAA, "My mom helped me a lot through puberty. She was very supportive and was good about answering my questions or even talking to me about things before I really even had questions."

Friends and Peers

Twenty participants reported having supportive friends and peers during adolescence. Friends and peers were supportive in numerous ways. Many participants remember sharing hygiene products with friends, practicing using makeup together, talking about sex and anatomy, discussing gender and sexuality experiences, and sharing hygiene and sexual tips. For RK, "My peers were generally supportive, even if inexperienced, and I did have other queer people at my school who I could talk to about stuff so I guess I was lucky in that regard." Some participants, like Nora, accessed books that their parents or peers' parents had: "I had a friend whose parents kept informational books about anatomy and sex for teenagers, and we would all go over and read them together and giggle."

Kate recalls, "When my friends and I talked about [puberty], it was mostly about skincare; just like comparing acne products and trying on all the samples at The Body Shop until we smelled revolting." In BA's experience, "My closest friends and I supported each other when we had our first periods." And for Shua, "For some reason, there's a 'girl code' when it comes to menstruation, and we would help each other out if someone was in need of sanitary products."

Some AFAB participants remember developing codes with other AFAB peers around menstruation, menstrual products, PMS, bras, and so forth. Rose, for example, "had a solid group of girls in middle school who were supportive. We developed our own secret language around bras and menstruation so that no one would know what we were talking about." Kae recalls, "Once we were all older, my friends had secret code words for period-related things." Some of these code words included "Aunt Flo is in town" to mean that one is on their period and "Can I borrow a pen?" to mean a request for a tampon.

Teachers and Other School Staff

One participant specifically mentioned having supportive teachers. Lane recalls, "I had two or three teachers that were very supportive of me and my coming out experience. I had a creative writing teacher who always used my preferred name when calling roll and always used they/them pronouns when referring to me, and did it really naturally, not calling it out. He also disciplined the jocks when they made fun of my pronouns. He'd call it out right away instead of waiting until after class to talk to them."

Queer-Specific Programming

Six participants had access to queer-affirming programming, either at school or in the community. These included Gender & Sexuality Alliances, Gay-Straight Alliances (both called GSAs), and Queer-Straight

Alliances (QSAs) at school and queer youth groups or events in the community. Lane, for example, attended the Gay-Straight Alliance at their school when they were questioning their gender identity: "The GSA opened my eyes. I knew I wasn't cis but I didn't know the terminology." Nora remembers, "I attended a queer youth group each week that was just life changing. It was facilitated by a trained team of all queer/trans adults who were truly invested in our lives and well-being. That is the place I felt most supported, by far." And for P, "I had no trans inclusive knowledge whatsoever until one GSA meeting in high school where a trans guy shared his story and everything finally clicked."

A safe space for an hour a week can genuinely change lives. According to a GLSEN research brief, "The presence of GSAs may help to make schools safer for LGBT students by sending a message that biased language and harassment will not be tolerated."[1] In addition, GSAs can help students locate supportive school staff, which increases the likelihood of academic achievement.[2]

UNSUPPORTIVE COMMUNITY MEMBERS

Sadly, more participants reported a lack of support from their communities. Lack of support included neglect, bullying, and abuse. Particularly for those youth who crossed gender boundaries by being masculine girls, feminine boys, or transgender, many were "encouraged by their parents to conform through gentle persuasion up through severe shaming and punishment and outright expulsion from the family."[3] These youth also faced scrutiny and violence from peers. According to a 2017 survey, transgender adolescents experience bullying and violence from peers at a rate of 80 percent.[4] Peer bullying and violence is especially heightened during middle and high school.

Bullying includes verbal harassment, physical harassment, physical assault, sexual harassment, relational aggression, electronic harassment or "cyberbullying," and property theft or damage at school.[5] Bullies target queer adolescents for sexual orientation, gender expression, and gender identity, as well as race, ethnicity, disability, and religion.[6]

Participants in this study experienced familial lack of support, including insistence on gender conformity, physical and sexual violence, stereotyping, neglect, and rejection. From peers, they received mockery, bullying, violence, and sexual harassment. From teachers and other school staff, they experienced invisibility in the classroom, covert support to bullies, refusal to use proper names and pronouns, and overt verbal bullying. From the wider society, they received targeted messages about compulsory cisnormative womanhood and manhood, heterosexual conformity, and expected future parenthood.

For many youths who transgress expected gender or sexual categories, secrecy and conformity become coping strategies. They then experience loneliness from self-isolation as well as distress from keeping such a monumental secret. In addition, participants who experienced lack of support from their communities tended to have a more difficult adolescence, higher rates of depression, more confusion about gender and sexual identity, and later coming out.

Family Members

Forty-six participants reported a lack of support from family members. This ranged from silences around gender and sexual identity to being kicked out of the house. Participants used words like "shame," "secretive," "abuse," and "stereotypes." Furthermore, two participants experienced nonconsensual genital surgery as children due to intersex features and were never told about it. They found out as adults upon accessing gender confirmation surgery.

Some participants experienced harsh expectations from parents and other family members. Skylar, for example, recalls, "My parents kept reinforcing that I was *supposed* to be uncomfortable, as a default, and I didn't understand that wanting to crawl out of my own skin because of my assigned gender wasn't normal." Other parents had unrealistic and bigoted assumptions; Isaako says, "My folks and family were very open and supportive of our sexual growth—as long as it was appropriately heterosexual and within our own class. I knew I wanted more, but I didn't know how to talk about it. I didn't really sort it all out until I left home." Some parents neglected or ignored this aspect of their children's lives. W remembers, "My parents were uncomfortable with those topics, and left me to my own devices."

Three participants discussed new rules that were suddenly created and enforced upon beginning puberty. B remembers, "All of a sudden there were all these rules that I didn't understand, that weren't there when I was a child. I didn't get why everything had to change just because I had breasts now." Nora's experience was similar: "My dad didn't take too long after puberty to start in on the misogynistic double standards about how I dressed or who I chose to befriend."

Some participants experienced parental violence. Some violence was sexual. In Rose's experience, "My father made lewd comments and molested me as I was going through my puberty. I thought it was my fault and tried to dress as unattractively as possible." Some violence was identity based. PA recalls, "My father used physical violence and talked down to me to suppress my gender nonconformity." For XA, "Family had strict gender roles, which only made puberty worse."

Both cisnormative masculinity and femininity were compulsory and enforced by some participants' family members. NAA remembers, "I was forced to dress, move, and behave in very feminine ways. From my early childhood up through my teen years, my father would physically hit me if he didn't think I was walking in a way that was feminine enough, or if I didn't sit in a way that was 'lady-like' enough." BA "would ask questions about gay people at home and my mom wouldn't usually answer. I was also told that I couldn't be a lesbian. She tried to sway me toward traditionally feminine clothing and activities."

Friends and Peers

Twenty-six participants reported a lack of support from friends and peers. This included alienation, stereotypes, teasing, bullying, and physical violence. Seven participants specifically mentioned stereotyping. Joe, for example, remembers,

> My peers were a more influential part of [puberty], primarily negative. First, there was the expectation that puberty meant girls were supposed to get larger breasts and mine really didn't get very large, so it meant I was less attractive to boys (insert eyeroll). Additionally, while boys were expected to and strived for more body hair, it was a source of shame and reason for mockery if girls had body hair. It resulted in myself, and most other girls I knew, shaving starting in middle school or early high school.

J dealt with stereotyping with stubbornness: "Sometimes I was shamed for not being feminine enough. But the little microaggression shame bullets just bounced right off me. I was too stubborn and self-confident to do anything different." Others had a harder time. G remembers, "I had very short hair, so my peers would mock me for having hair that contradicted my assigned gender identity. Male peers would snap my bra saying I shouldn't have it, or comment on my lack of 'balls' in my swimsuit. I regularly got mocked by my female peers for not shaving my legs and wearing only sports bras."

Some lessons were subtle. Seren says about her peers, "Sometimes I heard them say things about other people, and that's how I learned what I should or shouldn't try to do." Similarly, 'Uhane recalls, "My peers were not supportive, but I did learn from them. I learned how not to get their attention. I learned by observation how I ought to act, how I ought to behave, and how to remain invisible." Some participants felt isolated and lonely due to peer hostility. FAA remembers, "My peers made me feel super alienated because there was an inherent sense that I was different from them."

Several participants learned about compulsory heterosexuality from peers. Maddie learned about "homosexuality from my terrible school and my terrible homophobic classmates, which was not great. I had an incredibly warped idea of what it meant to be a lesbian for years." Isabelle remembers that "I learned through cultural osmosis that girls aren't supposed to be with girls and vice versa." ZA recalls, "I still remember my sophomore year when a less well-liked kid came out of the closet as gay and a kid openly threatened to drag him behind their truck with a chain."

Some participants experienced physical or sexual harassment from peers. For Rose, "I didn't hate my body until puberty. I experienced so much harassment in middle school from the boys that I stopped riding the bus, started dressing in baggy clothes, and refused to wear anything pink or 'girly.'" On the other hand, Cecily "got bullied/physically assaulted by other students on a daily basis. This is what prompted me to eventually start dressing more feminine and like the other girls, so I could blend in and maybe not be such a target."

Pubertal changes sparked a lot of harassment from peers for some participants. For LA, "I mainly learned grooming rules when people made fun of me for not following them. Like, I would hear, 'What? You don't shave your legs?' and come home and wonder if I should start shaving them." In PAA's experience, "Two girls who liked to harass everyone picked on me for having larger breasts." EA had a similar experience: "I was teased in fifth grade a lot by other girls because I was going through puberty."

Some peers were particularly cruel about menstrual management. A remembers "the constant anxiety of bleeding through my clothes or having someone catch me getting products from my bag. There was a lot of hate and disgust towards pads, they were compared to diapers and 'everyone' used tampons." Peers also focused on body hair and sexual practices; Q recalls, "Same-gender peers talked about how disgusting it was for girls to masturbate or have pubic hair so I felt lots of shame around that."

Teachers and Other School Staff

Several participants mentioned having unsupportive teachers. Lack of support included ignoring classmates bullying a queer youth, not using proper names and pronouns, excluding queer history from curricula, spreading misinformation about queer lives or focusing only on HIV risk, and bullying the youth explicitly. Sometimes, in response to peer bullying, teachers would tell the student to ignore the bullying or change their behavior to avert the bullying. Some teachers restricted queer expression by disciplining students for public displays of affection, telling them a queer logo violated the dress code, preventing them from discussing queer themes in school assignments, limiting queer content in extracurricular activities, or preventing them from playing sports.[7]

Wider Society

Aside from their more intimate communities, many participants received messages and lack of support from the wider society. This came in the form of television and advertisements that pushed for compulsory masculinity/femininity and heterosexuality, as well as stares and comments about gender expression. Seren, for example, "learned how I was 'supposed' to behave from TV shows. I didn't know I should ask my family questions." She learned how to be properly masculine, how to shave and use deodorant, and to be heterosexual and attract girls and women. Lane received direct instruction from people around them: "People would stare at me in the summer. They would give me judgmental looks for having long armpit and leg hair." Gender scrutiny and media messaging had a negative impact on many youth, particularly those transgressing gender norms.

6

EXPLORING GENDER

All of the transgender participants, two questioning participants, and two cisgender participants reported exploring their gender identities, some as early as preschool and some as late as midlife. This chapter investigates these experiences, focusing on the arrival of gendered self-knowledge; transition timelines or lack thereof; experiences of conformity, imposter syndrome, showing and hiding certain parts of their identities, and gender questioning; and community reactions.

SELF-KNOWLEDGE

Gender identity is a complex category. Many sociologists consider gender identity to be "a multidimensional construct that results from many factors, especially knowledge of one's membership in a particular gender category, sense of one's compatibility with that group, pressure to conform to the gender category, one's attitudes toward gender groups, and the centrality of one's gender relative to other identities."[1] Many participants discussed feelings of anxiety, confusion, and doubt about their assigned gender as well as hyperfocus on gendered behaviors. Some participants conformed to the gendered behaviors associated with their assigned gender, while others experimented with gender nonconformity.

Early: Preschool through Eighth Grade

Six participants reported self-awareness of their transgender identity sometime between preschool and eighth grade. Tommie Jayne was the youngest, at age three:

> I didn't know that I wasn't supposed to be a girl until the day before my sister's first birthday party. I wasn't quite four and was expecting to get my hair curled and my cousin's pink dress to wear. Instead, I was taken for my first of countless buzz cuts and dressed up in a really stupid looking sailor suit. My parents refused to listen to any of my complaints and they were hitters, so I shut up quickly and played along as best I could.

She wasn't the only participant who suppressed their gender identity after realizing it. Joe remembers,

> When I was around eight years old, Mulan came out and that was my first time feeling like 'yeah, these gender roles are ridiculous and suffocating me.' There was this connection to not being able to be a 'normal' girl nor a 'normal' boy but something else somewhere in the in-between. Unfortunately, it was quickly suppressed due to the lack of means of expressing any of these thoughts and not wanting to be any more different than I already was. I didn't start working on exploring and understanding my gender until my mid-twenties.

Mid: Ninth through Twelfth Grade

Seven participants reported coming to an awareness about their transgender identities in high school. Several of them were aided in their gender journeys by social media platforms like YouTube, Instagram, and Tumblr, where they could learn about other people's identities, explore their own, and form community.[2] Lane, for example, "learned about my gender identity from people on Instagram. Instagram and YouTube were my outlets for looking up my identity and then finding people who were like me." FAA also gained self-knowledge via social media: "I suppressed my identity for a very long time. There were a few times where I was so close to realizing it, but I just repressed it again because of the inconvenient timing. I didn't actually accept it until halfway through tenth grade. I spent my time watching other trans people on TV and YouTube and I felt a strong bond I couldn't explain."

Suppression of gender identity was a common theme. EAA clung to assigned gender conformity: "Around the time I was sixteen [or] seventeen, I was pretty sure I wasn't 'right.' All the praying in the world wasn't going to 'fix' what was wrong with me. So I suppressed, and leaned into hyperfemme a bit." Similarly, HA recalls, "I always felt more like a boy than a girl, and was called tomboy a lot. From puberty on I felt like I was split in two, like I was trying to kill part of myself off every day. It is only in the last month that I have accepted I am nonbinary. For the first time in my life I don't feel split in two!"

Some participants experimented with cross-dressing in adolescence but suppressed and didn't connect it to gender identity until later in life. Erin, for example, remembers:

> I never really understood my gender identity growing up. I did experiment when I was an adolescent with my mom's clothes and makeup. I remember being turned on by it. That was forgotten through my teens and I grew up as a boy because that's the identity that was given to me. It wasn't until I learned about transgender people that it made me question myself. I lived in denial through my twenties trying to just live a heterosexual life. It wasn't until my divorce in my thirties that made me realize I should start working on it, really figuring it out. So now I'm ten months into transitioning in my mid-thirties.

Later: Post–High School

Most (25) transgender participants reported gender awareness after high school, some long after. Some had felt vaguely uncomfortable for much of their early lives without realizing why. For others, it was like a switch had flipped when they realized they were transgender. Most probed their early memories for "evidence" that they had been gender nonconforming in some way. Some participants remember that they were perfectly comfortable as "eggs"[3] before gaining self-awareness of their gender identities.

Many older participants didn't realize they were transgender as youth because they had never been exposed to the concept. For V, "being uneducated about transgender issues set me back a while discovering my identity. Being a woman was always something that would be amazing, but never could happen." B remembers, "Until Chaz Bono, I had no idea that FTM[4] even existed." Shua says, "It took me years to ever find out about the LGBT community, and once I did, I finally put all the pieces together and claimed my identity!"

Some participants didn't think they could be transgender because they didn't see their particular identity or expression represented in media or within their communities. For LAA, "I chose a college that was known for having a strong queer presence, which was great for learning about different identities and getting more comfortable with the idea that queerness is common, but many of the trans/nonbinary people I met were very different from how I saw myself, which possibly pushed me away from those identities until I was well into my twenties."

TRANSITION TIMING

Transition is a complex, personal affair. Timelines are completely individual; people pick and choose options at their own pace. Some people have the good fortune to begin their transitions before the age of eighteen, while others wait until midlife or later. Some medical transition elements for transfeminine people include estrogen therapy, breast augmentation, facial feminization surgery, orchiectomy,[5] and vaginoplasty.[6] Some transition elements for transmasculine people include testosterone therapy, mastectomy[7] and chest reshaping, oophorectomy,[8] hysterectomy,[9] and metoidioplasty.[10] Some people choose one or more of these elements, while others choose not to take any of these medical steps. Sometimes choice is constrained by finances, health, age, the law, and/or community support.

Transition is not solely a medical journey. Social transition involves coming out to oneself and others, sometimes changing one's name and/ or pronouns, and sometimes altering one's gender expression. Legal transition involves legally changing one's name and/or sex on birth certificates, driver's licenses, and other vital records and documents. As with medical transition, not all trans people pursue social or legal transition, with the same constraints. For a deeper discussion of transition, see chapter 9.

Early: Before Age Eighteen

Three participants reported starting their gender transitions before the age of eighteen. For prepubescent and pubescent youth, with consent from parents, hormone blockers are a possibility. This allows the youth to explore their gender identity without puberty changing their bodies irrevocably. Then, when they are certain, they can discontinue hormone blockers and either go through natural puberty or begin hormone replacement therapy. However, none of the participants in this study had access to hormone blockers. Instead, they began social transition and some began hormone replacement therapy in their later teens.

Mid: Age Eighteen through Thirty

Seven participants reported starting their gender transitions between the ages of eighteen and thirty. For those who had earlier self-knowledge, they put off transition for many reasons: transphobic or potentially transphobic family or guardians, not yet being financially independent, abusive relationships, imposter syndrome, lack of information about transition, and identity suppression. Seren experienced imposter syndrome: "I felt like I wasn't good enough to be a woman. I so respected and felt a connection to women and femmes around me, I felt a familiarity and respect, but I thought, *I'm not them, I'm not as good as them, I have to be as good as them to be a woman*." Then, when she finally started hormone replacement therapy, "I felt that peace that I only felt momentarily; suddenly, I was feeling it all the time. My body needed this the whole time and it finally got it. I'm going forward in life knowing who I am and knowing what my goals are and happy to finally be the person I want to be."

T lacked access to transition information for a long time. "I was not exposed to the opportunity to transition until I was twenty-three. I stumbled across a guy that had had top surgery on Instagram. I then connected with a guy that lived in the same state as me at the time and he told me where to get testosterone." Some participants suppressed their identities for a period of time before coming out and transitioning. W "learned to pass as a 'man' and repressed until I was twenty-two. I was close to killing myself, so I decided to transition instead. I'm glad I did!" G had a relationship that hindered their ability to explore: "I actively suppressed my more masculine tendencies, 'helped' by an un-healthy relationship that fulfilled the Christian expectations of being a dutiful female partner and deferring to the man's preferences."

Others transitioned after a period of experimentation. LA, for example, "figured out I was trans after a trans friend and leader of our queer community died. As a way of mourning, I became as openly queer as possible, to make up for the hole they left. So I cut my hair short (which I've wanted to do for ages), and got a binder (which I heard about from a cosplay group), and got some shorts from the boys' section. And a funny thing happened. I noticed that I really wanted to be 'mistaken for a boy.' So I investigated it and played around with my pronouns and coming out to my friends, and discovered I was quite happy being a guy."

Later: Over Age Thirty

Nine participants reported starting their gender transitions after age thirty. This was mostly due to the same reasons mentioned above. Christina experimented with dressing in women's clothing long before she actually came out and began her transition:

> I started dressing up, every Halloween, for parties. I enjoyed it. Still, folks would laugh at me. I just kind of pretended I was joking about it. I tried to be a man and raise a family, but began to experience PTSD. I wasn't myself . . . . I knew I had to awaken a dormant part of me to survive. But the fear and anxiety has been overwhelming. But it feels so good and free and *right* to be me. Coming out has been so hard, but so rewarding. I can never go back in the closet, I'm ready to be myself full-time forever.

B also repressed their identity: "I tried *really* hard to be a good woman and do everything I was 'supposed' to. I clumsily stomped through womanhood, checking all the boxes. I grew my hair long, I spit out a bunch of kids, I had my nails done, I let my husband beat me and struggled to submit to him like I had been taught. I was miserable, and really bad at it."

EXPERIENCES

This section discusses some common themes among participants. Many participants attempted to conform to their assigned gender. Some, like Seren, experienced imposter syndrome. Many suppressed their identities or chose to show or hide parts of their identities at different times or with different people. And some people questioned or are still questioning their gender identities.

Attempts to Conform

Many participants attempted to conform to their assigned gender before coming out and transitioning. Seventeen used the word "suppress" to articulate their conformity experience. They suppressed their gender identities for various reasons: family, friends, religion, workplace, and so forth. Five specifically mentioned that they "tried to be a good cis"—in other words, to conform to societal and familial expectations of their assigned genders through "opposite-sex" marriage, having children, or engaging in behaviors and careers that were highly gendered (for example, nurses, nannies, and housewives for AFAB participants; military, police officers, and firefighters for AMAB participants).[11]

In an example above, participant B followed the path of "traditional womanhood" by marrying a man, having children, and staying in an abusive relationship. EAA was religious and tried to literally "pray the trans away." And HA articulated "splitting themselves in two" in order to conform and suppress their nonbinary identity. These attempts to conform may have kept participants relatively safe with families and friendships intact, but they wreaked havoc on their psyches. Children and adolescents in particular see quite clearly the societal messages telling them to conform to gendered expectations, and often must suppress in order to remain safe and housed. Those who do not conform sufficiently are beleaguered by peer bullying and resulting depression, anxiety, and isolation.

Imposter Syndrome

Some participants experienced imposter syndrome: not feeling "trans enough" or not being validated in their gender. This was most common among nonbinary people who have a gender expression similar to that of their assigned gender and binary trans people who are not successful at passing.[12] Anytime someone is told that they look like their assigned gender rather than their true gender, it feels invalidating and can cause gender dysphoria as well as depression, anxiety, and isolation.

Above, Seren reported feeling like she could never be as good as the women in her life and therefore couldn't be a real woman. She describes the affection, admiration, and respect she feels for women, while considering herself less-than. And LAA was pushed away from developing a trans identity because they didn't see themselves reflected in their community or in media; they assumed they couldn't be trans since their experience looked and felt different.

Showing and Hiding Identities

Most, if not all, transgender people make choices on a regular basis about whether to be open about their identities and experiences. Sometimes this means coming out to some people but not others, or being fully out but not bothering to correct the grocery store clerk about pronouns; sometimes this means selectively showing parts of their identity but not others, or coming out little by little over time.

Manumalo was very strategic about developing their expression and coming out: "My journey was careful and calculated. I needed to be financially independent to bring myself to a point where I initially came out as a femme lesbian. Then I slowly became more androgynous appearing. I gradually started to purchase men's clothing and then cut my hair short. Now, I identify as a butch lesbian, masculine of center presenting, and fa'atane expressly."

Questioning

Four participants are currently (as of this research) questioning their gender identities, and two explored their gender identities and subsequently realized that they were cisgender. RK, for example, "did consider my gender and relationship to gender performance throughout high school, but I always ended up feeling masculinity fit me best." Similarly, J says that "being androgynous and masculine as a woman I did go for many years as a no-hormone trans nonbinary person using he/

she/they pronouns all of them always. I have gone back to identifying as cis and more like a woman than trans or nonbinary anymore."

Questioning can be a poignant time for some participants, filled with self-doubt and confusion. For Kate, "I thought about being a boy a lot for a cis girl, but that didn't seem relevant. Now I'm in my early thirties, and it's never stopped, and it's feeling more and more relevant, but also my life is good now and change is scary, and what if I'm just appropriating an identity that doesn't belong to me, and *internal screaming*." Rose recalls, "The only time I felt distressed was when people started talking about being a woman. I thought that menarche was what made you a woman, but some people said that childbirth made you a woman. Others said that turning eighteen made you a woman. I couldn't figure it out, and no one could answer me when I asked exactly what it means to be a woman."

COMMUNITY REACTIONS

Particularly for younger participants, family and community have a major role in one's gender journey. Assigned gender nonconformity is generally a source of surprise and interest. This can turn into either support or lack thereof. Supportive families told their children they could be whatever they wanted to be and supported exploration in identity and expression. Unsupportive families forced their children into gendered behaviors and expression and sometimes punished them quite severely for straying from conformity. For older participants, community reactions could be just as helpful or damaging. The difference between tolerance and transphobia can mean having or losing a job, acquiring or being denied housing, being celebrated or bashed.

Supportive Community Members

Five participants reported having supportive community members during their gender journeys: support came from family, friends, and mentors. Support from family involved acceptance or tolerance of the nonnormative gender identity or expression, purchasing their children gender-affirming clothing, and taking them to queer youth meetings and events. More subtle support included using the person's chosen name and pronouns and acknowledging their transition and new life and friends. Support from friends included unconditional love, talking through issues and questions, standing up against bullies, and using the proper name and pronouns. Support from mentors involved creating a safe space at school for the youth to be themselves without question. Lane, for example, had a teacher who always used their pronouns and corrected other students in class.

Unsupportive Community Members

Seven participants reported a lack of support from community members during their gender journeys; this included both family and peers. Lack of support can directly lead to adverse health outcomes, including "higher risks of poorer health outcomes including substance use, eating disorders, suicidality, risky sexual behaviors, exposure to violence, victimization, and homelessness."[13] Other health concerns for transgender youth include smoking, HIV, and hepatitis from injection hormones, silicone, and street drugs.[14]

Sometimes families were unsupportive due to ignorance. Without a shared minority experience, families were often confused and youth were uncertain about their parents' ability to protect or understand them.[15] And families sometimes had external reasons to be non-affirming: "cultural institutions such as churches and communities that advocate intolerance and, in turn, reject parents and families if they tolerate [transgender] behavior."[16] Participants B and G both experienced unhealthy relationships with partners who rejected their gender nonconformity. Lane's father forced them to stop going to their school's GSA. Christina got laughed at when she dressed up for Halloween. Lack of support and intolerance can result in depression, anxiety, isolation, and delayed gender exploration and coming out.

7

EXPLORING SEXUALITY

Sexual orientation is a term describing one's physical and/or romantic attractions.[1] All of the cisgender participants and most of the transgender participants in this survey reported exploring their sexual identities, some as early as preschool and some as late as midlife. Most exploration occurred after a period of self-imposed conformity to heterosexual behavior or stated identity. This chapter investigates the ways in which participants came to realize their sexual identities and explore them, focusing on the arrival of non-heterosexual self-knowledge, personal experiences such as attempts to conform and internalized queerphobia, and community reactions to participants' sexual identities.

SELF-KNOWLEDGE

Due to compulsory girlhood/boyhood and heteronormativity, people are presumed to be heterosexual until proven otherwise. This is part of why coming out can be so fraught; it positions non-heterosexual sexual identities as non-normative and something that must be announced to be believed or seen. The normalization of heterosexuality and lack of discussion and resources about non-heterosexual identities also means that many queer youth assume that they must be heterosexual until they come to the realization that they are not. Even in cases where a youth has an obvious crush on somebody of the same sex, they often chalk it up to youthful confusion or experimentation and hold off on coming to terms with their non-heterosexual identity until later in life.

Early: Preschool through Eighth Grade

Twenty-eight participants reported self-discovery of a non-heterosexual identity between preschool and eighth grade. These participants tended to skew younger and therefore had access to the Internet as well as other media resources that helped them understand LGBTQIA+ identities and experiences at a younger age than older participants, who had very few or no resources at these ages.

A large number of participants came to realize their queer identity via popular culture representations, including movies, television, music, books, video and computer games, and social media. Z, for example, "realized I was attracted to women when I was twelve. I was a little confused about it, but would research it online and watch shows like *Degrassi* and *South of Nowhere* and that helped me understand it." Others had crushes. Nora remembers, "I have always had crushes on women. I was in Girl Scouts for twelve years and I can remember even at five years old that every summer there was one girl I just couldn't forget about, and I just wanted to think about her face."

Mid: Ninth through Twelfth Grade

Likewise, many high school–aged realizers discovered their sexual identities via popular culture. Twenty-eight participants became aware of their non-heterosexual sexual identities between ninth and twelfth grade. X, for example, recalls,

> At sixteen, I was playing *Assassin's Creed: Black Flag* and at the time James Kidd was my favorite character. He was striking and I found him incredibly attractive. Then, later in the game, it is revealed that James Kidd was a Mary Read all along and had disguised herself as a man. I was shook. I was a little betrayed but ultimately I was confused because I still found her attractive. It sparked a lot of questioning.

Kate tells a similar story:

> I actually came out to myself while watching a loaned copy of *But I'm a Cheerleader*. When Natasha Lyonne said, "Everyone reads 'Cosmo,' everyone looks at other girls all the time," and another character says, "But you only assume they're thinking what you're thinking," she looked shocked and I bet I looked even more shocked. I spent the rest of the movie in a state of "Oh fuck."

And Ellie remembers, "I was unaware of the term bisexual until about 2005. I watched the film *Frida* and learned about Frida Kahlo. That is how I came to realize that bisexuality was a real identity and it was who I was."

Participant A also achieved self-discovery through popular culture, specifically a television show: "I would have to say that *Buffy the Vampire Slayer* played a big part in realizing that my crushes on girls were crushes. The show and others also helped me discover bisexuality and later pansexuality." Not only did she realize her own sexuality, she also learned about others through watching popular media. Others took solace from popular culture representations. J recalls, "I grew up with *Rocky Horror* and Queen and seeing a lot of that mainstream gender skirting stuff and so I think I knew from a young age that it existed and I just needed to be patient."

Later: Post–High School

The majority of participants (35) realized their non-heterosexual identities after high school. While younger participants and those who discovered their sexualities younger more frequently came to their discoveries via popular culture, some older participants also found popular culture illuminating in their sexuality journeys. Asexual adults in particular often utilized the internet to learn about asexuality and identify themselves as such. DA, for example, remembers, "When I was twenty, I came across a post on the internet about asexuality, and that was when things really started clicking. I think I realized I was asexual over the course of both one night and about eight months."

Similarly, CA "learned about asexuality on the internet my freshman year of college, and I realized that I was asexual. It was incredible to realize that I wasn't broken for not being interested in sex." And G recalls that "[a friend] posted a meme from an asexual Facebook page and I went, 'Wait . . . that's *me!*' I did a lot more research online, went on the AVEN website, talked to my boyfriend/best friend, and came out as asexual."

Others discovered their sexual identities through friends and peers. Seren, for example, "learned about non-heterosexual identities mostly from my roommates when I went to college." It was partially through these friendships that she discovered her own queerness. Most participants who came to their identities after high school made the discovery through having a crush or engaging in sexual experimentation. Participant I says, "I definitely think of my queer journey starting with being attracted to a specific person."

EXPERIENCES

There were several common themes in terms of specific experiences with sexual identity formation. Many participants attempted to conform to heterosexual expectations, some for only a short while and some for years. Many experienced imposter syndrome, or not feeling queer enough in some way. Quite a few participants, mostly bisexuals and asexuals, experienced invisibility and erasure. Most participants made conscious decisions to show some parts of their identity and hide others, to gradually reveal more over time, or to reveal to some people but not others. And many experienced confusion and questioning during their journey, with a few participants still questioning at the time of this research.

Attempts to Conform

Many participants attempted to conform to traditional heterosexual expectations for some amount of time. They used words and phrases like "I suppressed it" (33), "closeted" (12), and "tried to choose to be straight" (9). Those who suppressed their non-heterosexual identities did so due to being in an opposite-sex relationship, family expectations or homophobia, religious faith, and fear and anxiety. Some participants experienced internalized homophobia/biphobia and hated themselves for being queer or believed popular negative stereotypes about queer people.

Maddie remembers, "I did a really great job of pushing my feelings way, way, way down deep into my 'mind vault' so that whenever I had an intrusive thought like 'Megan has nice boobs' I'd interrupt it with something else." Similarly, Peri "first caught myself staring at the (rather large) chest of a classmate when I was in sixth grade. Right about the time my hormones went haywire. I panicked. I freaked out because anyone who wasn't straight was demonized in the South. I didn't want that." Likewise, FAA "had a huge crush on one of my best girl friends when I was eight, but I felt like it was wrong because that's what I was taught my whole life. I then proceeded to suppress it until I was about fifteen or so."

Some participants tried their best to be straight. PAA recalls, "In elementary school, in an effort to fit in, I would just randomly select a boy to have a fake crush on. I think I tried that twice, partly just wanting to have something to talk to the other kids about and partly thinking that maybe if I chose one of them I would start to develop genuine feelings. Of course, it never stopped being totally forced." O had a similar experience: "Being bisexual specifically is weird because you can coast on being attracted to the people you're 'supposed' to be. I remember thinking about guys occasionally in high school and freaking out, shutting it down, thinking Satan was trying to get a foothold of some kind."

Religion was a factor for many participants. They had been taught that homosexuality was a sin. For WA,

> When people called me gay I went in the closet because gay was "gross," "sin," "unnatural," and "womanly." I started acting as "manly" as possible, getting in fights and being a toxic jerk. *Glee* was the show that taught me about gay men. It was what convinced me it was okay for other people to be gay. It wasn't until my senior year of high school I started thinking I wasn't straight. It was actually an anime called *Yuri on Ice* that helped me view my sexuality as normal.

Others suppressed due to social status. S remembers, "When I got to college and met girls who identified as lesbians, I quickly realized how much I related to them. But my social circle was very cis/hetero and I didn't want to lose my social status so I kept it to myself and kept pursuing guys. Once I graduated and started my career, I finally worked up the nerve to come out and start dating women for real." Others experienced internalized homophobia/biphobia. Jack "definitely suppressed my attraction to men in every way for many years. I had deeply inset homophobia from years of just hating on gay men mostly. For some reason, all the funniest jokes of the '90s and '00s was just gay people as the punchline I guess."

Many participants experienced pressure from loved ones to be properly heterosexual. DAA had a college girlfriend who "told me early on that if she ever found out I was bisexual then she would break up with me. I felt like there was no reason to ever express who I was. I repressed it so hard that I never allowed myself to even think a homosexual thought."

Some participants suppressed very passively. JAA, for example, "knew I was into men in my late teens. In hindsight, I was also into women, but compulsory heterosexuality made it easy to ignore mild crushes." Similarly, participant I remembers that "as a young person, I was passively suppressing my queerness. There were moments as I was beginning to realize I was queer when I then pushed those feelings down . . . . I know that there were queer attractions that I felt before that I intentionally put out of my mind." Seren, on the other hand, "never suppressed my identity consciously, but I was so busy trying to find companionship I didn't have much time to really explore who I was until very recently."

Imposter Syndrome, Invisibility, and Erasure

Some participants experienced imposter syndrome. Specifically, bisexual and asexual participants often felt "not queer enough" in some way. Some bisexuals even felt that their sexuality didn't matter if they were in an opposite-sex relationship. Others weren't aware of bisexuality as an orientation and used their opposite-sex attraction as proof of straightness. Jack recalls, "By some point toward the end of high school, I was actively self-denying any possibility of being gay since 'well, I like women, so I can't be gay,' since I guess the term bisexual (or biromantic) hadn't entered my vocabulary." Similarly, BAA "never really knew bisexuality was real until I experienced it. It was never represented and when it was people would say they were confused. Since I knew I was attracted to boys I thought I had to be straight."

Imposter syndrome is deeply connected to invisibility and erasure, which many bisexuals and asexuals experience, even within the queer community. HAA's experience is that

> because of bi invisibility, I went back and forth for a while debating whether I was "just gay" or "just straight." I wasn't even familiar with the term "bisexual" growing up, so I never knew it was an option until much later. There weren't role models for me, and the few examples of queer people I saw were either hyperfeminine gay men or hypermasculine lesbians, neither of which I could personally identify with.

Among twelve participants who had experienced invisibility and erasure, HAA's experience is ubiquitous. F, for example, "ended up being confused if I was a lesbian in denial or a hetero experimenting because I had no idea that bi/pan was a real thing (never had heard the term pan; bi was deemed not real when I was growing up)."

Showing and Hiding Identities

Most participants, at some point in their lives, made conscious decisions to both show and hide their identities. Some showed parts of their identity but not their complete identity, some started sharing just a little and gradually shared more and more, and some disclosed their identity to some people and not others. These strategies make sense because being out can be very dangerous. Showing some parts of identity (such as being bisexual) but not others (such as being transgender) can keep a person safer in places where bisexuality is widely accepted but trans identities are still faced with hostility.[2] Starting by sharing a little and then gradually sharing more and more can help somebody discern if they can trust the person they are sharing with. And being out to some people but not others makes sense when a person knows they have support from some but would be spurned by others. "Many LGBTQ youths and adults are often selective about disclosure of sexual orientation. In fact, most LGBTQs are not out to everyone in all settings."[3]

Confusion and Questioning

Most participants reported feeling confused about their sexual orientation or questioning it, particularly participants who developed a same-sex attraction at a young age. Seven participants were unable to decipher their sexual orientation until they realized they were transgender or non-cisgender in some way. V remembers, "I always knew I was queer, just didn't know how due to presenting as the wrong gender my whole life." For LAA, "I had a lot of trouble differentiating between people I was attracted to and people I envied for a long time. I did not decide I was bi until adulthood, but that happened once I definitively realized I was not a ciswoman—coming to grips with my gender identity made me able to figure out what was happening with my sexual identity as well."

Three participants thought that all women looked at other women. For Rose, "it never occurred to me that I might actually be bisexual—in fact, it felt almost imperative to my survival that I remain unambiguously heterosexual. I thought that all women enjoyed looking at other women and it was just a normal part of being a heterosexual woman." And many participants didn't initially recognize same-sex attractions as such. Shua recalls, "I would always be attracted to girls, but didn't even know that I liked them in that way. I don't know why. Maybe it was from societal pressures that everyone is heterosexual by default."

Asexual participants had a particularly difficult time coming to terms with their identities.[4] Fifteen had no awareness of asexuality until learning much later. Four articulated that they truly believed that everybody around them was making it (sexual attraction) all up. Aly, for example, "went on dates, kissed some people, but nothing felt quite right. That's when I started doing more research and stumbled upon asexuality as a description for my feelings."

Others had more extensive experimental phases. RK remembers,

> I had some hookups, tried kink, tried an orgy, etc. but couldn't figure out why I wasn't feeling the lust other people clearly felt. This contributed to a fairly severe bout of depression. Sometime in that time, I must have googled something that brought me around to a description of asexuality because I just remember staying up all night and reading about all these people who'd experienced the exact same thing as me. I hate hyperbolic "huge weight lifted from my shoul-

ders" kind of statements but it really was pretty much like that and I came out publicly later that week. I finally felt comfortable in my sexuality, and in my own skin.

Many asexual participants reported feeling abnormal prior to the discovery of asexuality as an orientation. For AAA, "Most of my growing up was just dealing with the fact that I was weird and different. I learned about asexuality in college and from the get-go it felt so right, like there were finally other people who understood how I felt."

Some female asexual participants had been raised with the idea that women didn't experience sexual desire. They were left feeling confused upon discovering that this wasn't the case. In church, NAA was "taught that women didn't naturally want sex. It took me until adulthood to figure out I was demisexual because I was taught that that's just the way I as an AFAB person was supposed to be."

COMMUNITY REACTIONS

Family and community have a significant impact on the well-being of queer people as they discover and explore their sexualities. Some people demonstrate queer signs at a young age. For those who were supported by family and community, they generally experienced an easier time on their journey. For those who were not supported, they experienced forced conformity, verbal bullying, physical and sexual violence, intolerance from religious institutions, and homelessness. For older participants experiencing community rejection, experiences ranged from bullying and violence to job and housing instability.

Supportive Community Members

Sadly, a mere eighteen participants reported having supportive community members as they discovered and explored their sexualities. Three had supportive families, five had supportive friends, and ten had supportive older mentors. Isaako had one such mentor: "I grew up in San Francisco, and even in the 1960s, gay liberation was a common topic of casual conversation. My best friend in high school's Dad was gay and was an excellent role model." Unfortunately, no other participants discussed in depth the ways in which their communities were supportive, other than articulating love and care from family, actions of allyship from friends, and advice from mentors.

Unsupportive Community Members

Sixteen participants reported negative reactions and lack of support from their communities, including family and peers. Participants who began exploring their sexual identities at younger ages often experienced bullying from peers, especially at school. They also experienced pushback from family members, particularly parents. Some families were tentatively supportive about some aspects of their child's sexuality but unsupportive about other things. For Lane, "My dad was okay with me dating girls, but didn't want me to show affection to my girlfriend in front of my younger household members and my conservative step-grandma."

For some participants, homophobia was so engrained in their cultural milieu that they took on the burden of internalizing it. Most frequently, casual homophobia such as using the term "gay" as an insult had a major impact on participants' journeys of sexual orientation discovery and exploration. Joe remembers that

> the term "gay" was the first queer word I heard and there was nothing positive about it. It was used to express people's disinterest in an activity or to emasculate boys. Having no vocabulary or representation for what I was experiencing, I quickly internalized a lot of the negativity surrounding being "gay," filling up with shame and self-hatred which resulted in a deep depression and my first suicide attempt by halfway through the seventh grade.

GA also experienced self-loathing due to homophobic remarks: "I had always known what being gay meant, and I knew it was bad. My parents said mean things about gay people, it was an insult and a joke to kids. Any time I found myself thinking gay thoughts I'd panic. I realized in high school I was bi, but never planned on dating girls. If I was bi, I thought I could just date men and basically be straight." Others experienced targeted homophobia from their religious communities. NAA, for example, "first heard about gay people at church: specifically, in a sermon that condemned them." And HA "used to hate myself for being bisexual and believed I was going to hell. It is only within the last year that I have been able to reconcile my sexual orientation and faith."

While none of my participants reported being kicked out of their family home for their sexual orientation, this is sadly a common reality for many queer youth. Queer youth are overrepresented in homeless shelters and camps,[5] where they are at a higher risk for substance abuse, risky sexual behaviors, pregnancy, prostitution, HIV and other sexually transmitted infections, suicide, and abuse and assault by homophobic peers and older community members.[6] Trauma from physical, sexual, and verbal violence often results in negative mental health outcomes, including post-traumatic stress disorder.[7] Family and peer support can make all the difference in a queer youth's life as they figure out and become confident with their sexual orientation.

8

COMING OUT

Coming out is a rite of passage wherein an LGBTQIA+ individual first acknowledges their queerness to themself and then discloses to others, typically friends and family members, but sometimes to all within the individual's social milieu. Self-identification is a vital step to self-affirmation and affinity with a minoritized community. Coming out "constitutes a process of self-discovery and personal identity-building that alters the way one comes to view [themself] and carries profound contextual implications."[1] However, coming out can also be a frustrating experience because of cisheterosexual presumption; being socialized and raised in a cisheteronormative environment means that youth are expected to be cisgender and heterosexual.[2]

Coming out is often challenging. Consequences can range from disapproval from family and friends to housing and job insecurity. However, positive aspects can include love, support, and allyship from community members. In addition, coming out can result in better health, including "less stress and fewer symptoms of depression and anxiety, higher self-esteem, increases in strength and courage and improved social skills."[3] This chapter explores the ways in which participants came out (or chose not to) and the community reactions they received.

TIMING

Data show that LGBTQIA+ people come out earlier on average than they did in the past. In the 1970s the average age of coming out was twenty-one years old. Now most people come out in their teens.[4] For younger cohorts, new media were a way to practice queer identification and coming out before coming out IRL.[5] For example, many younger participants explicitly mentioned learning about queer identities on YouTube, Reddit, and other social media. They used these platforms both to learn about queer identities as well as to build community, create content, and try out different identities using avatars and profile information. And for younger cohorts, LGBTQIA+ identification and coming out generally came before sexual exploration, whereas previous cohorts often experimented before declaring an identity.[6]

Early: Preschool through Eighth Grade

Six participants reported coming out of the closet before high school. Zoe, for example, "came out to friends in middle school/junior high. I came out to my family later on but they seemed like they already knew when I mentioned it, and it wasn't really a formal coming out. Now I identify proudly and openly as queer so even my distant family and acquaintances know this about me." This experience is quite common; most participants came out first to a trusted friend before coming out to family.[7]

Mid: Ninth through Twelfth Grade

Twenty-three participants reported coming out of the closet during high school. Some of them had an astonishingly easy time with it. J "had two girlfriends in high school. We kissed in the halls. Went to prom. I was never gay bashed." Others received some backlash from those to whom they came out. For CJ, "My dad did say something to the effect of, 'That's what every teenager would say and we'll see how you feel when you're older,' but it's been like four years and I haven't so . . ." Most participants who came out while still living with their parents were very strategic, only coming out because they felt safe enough to.

Later: Post–High School to Age Thirty

The majority (58) of participants came out during the period between the end of high school and age thirty. For some, they carefully waited until they were moved out and financially secure before coming out to family. T, for example, "came out later in life when I was financially stable in case my family disowned me." Similarly, NAA "didn't come out to anyone until adulthood for safety reasons." Others waited until they had an external reason to come out. Isaako was one of these: "I was lucky to know Harvey Milk when I was in my twenties. I bought my film from him and voted for him every chance I got. When he was murdered I made a commitment to live openly, as a way to honor his memory. I was the first openly queer man to work at most of my jobs, and I always took that responsibility very seriously." Most of these participants waited until they had someone special in their lives to come out. It was easy to remain closeted before that, but once they had a sweetheart, they decided to be open. For S, "I came out at twenty-four. Per the advice of a lesbian friend, I waited until I had someone in my life worth coming out for."

Participants who came out during this time were also often waiting until they were physically safe (i.e., away from family or other aggressors) to come out. In addition, many had years of internalized queerphobia to challenge before coming out. Joe was one of these:

> I didn't come out until later in life for a few reasons. The first being that I lacked the support and vocabulary to discuss my queerness. There was little to no representation of the queer community in my life that I could look to for support or explanations. I also held off on coming out until late in life because I was ashamed of who I was. There was a lot of built up internalized homophobia that caused me to hate myself and that part of me, so I kept it hidden. Lastly, there was fear. I feared that people would hate me and that I would lose any sense of support or social comfort. I also feared physical and emotional harm from others who didn't understand because I had seen it happen to another and was scared of meeting the same fate.

Finally, some participants waited to come out because they didn't recognize their queerness until later. Maddie, for example, "realized I was gay when I was twenty-one, and dated a man briefly. It really shook me to my core when I finally realized how profoundly wrong it felt. It made me reevaluate a lot of things. I came out to everyone in my life on Facebook when I was twenty-two."

Much Later: After Age Thirty

Eleven participants reported coming out of the closet after age thirty. Most of these were from earlier cohorts who had lived through the criminalization of their gender identities or sexual orientations. Many did not feel safe coming out in that cultural milieu, but once awareness and tolerance began to increase, they were able to come out. Several bisexual participants did not come out until later because they were in opposite-sex relationships and didn't feel the need to. QA's experience was that "I came out recently in my thirties. For most of my life I just ignored that piece of my identity. It was easy to do because I married a man and it didn't seem like an option to explore with women. So I just shut it off." Some transgender participants also waited to come out due to fears around safety and comfort. For Erin, "I didn't come out until I was thirty-three. I didn't come out because I had suppressed it for a long time and was scared of the ramifications with my family and work."

EXPERIENCES

No participants came out to every single person in their life at the same time. Instead, some chose to come out slowly over time to a widening circle. A few came out multiple times, for example, first as gay and later as pansexual. Many chose to come out to some people but not others. And some participants have remained closeted for safety or other reasons. It's important to note that coming out isn't a one-time experience. Somebody who chooses to be out to all in their lives must come out repeatedly every time they meet a new person due to the automatic assumption of cisgender heterosexuality.[8]

Coming Out over Time

Twenty-one participants reported coming out of the closet over time. In fact, the most common pattern of disclosure was first to a trusted friend, then to family. Sometimes this process is fairly quick, and other times it takes years. Z recalls, "I told my best friend when we were seventeen. I came out to my mom before I went to college and came out to the rest of the family a couple years later." JAA was likewise strategic about when and to whom to disclose:

> Once I started considering I was trans, I spent probably a year or so privately going back and forth about it, came out as "probably not a woman" to my boyfriend and best friend, then started seeing a therapist to figure stuff out. From there I came out as "somewhat transmasculine" to my friends, and eventually as a trans man to my family shortly before starting on T. Once I got on T, I planned to wait until I was regularly passing to strangers before coming out at work, but after nearly a year that wasn't happening and not being out at work was getting to me, so I came out there and am now out everywhere in my life.

X also thought carefully about who to come out to and when:

> I came out to my gay family friend and he advised me to come out to my mom before I went off to college. I came out to the rest of my straight high school friends when I got a girlfriend in college. I didn't want to come out to them [before] because they were straight women who I thought might get weird around me and I didn't want to lose their friendship because they thought I was hitting on them or something.

Coming Out Multiple Times

There were many participants who identified as more than one LGBTQIA+ identity or started identifying as one and then realized they identified as another. Twenty-one of these participants came out multiple times, first as one identity, then as another. Seren, for example, first came out as nonbinary, then as a trans woman, and then as a lesbian: "I slowly uncovered layers for my parents. I was just open as much as I could be with friends." Erin also came out first as nonbinary and then as a transgender woman. K recalls, "I have come out multiple times. First it was telling people I'm queer, then telling them what pronouns I wanted them to use." For Manumalo, "I came out at twenty-two, then again in my early thirties. With my current physical presentation, folks might glean that my sexual orientation is not in a heteronormative binary context."

Some folks experienced easy and supportive coming out as one identity but not another. RK had one such experience:

> During adolescence I came out as a bisexual, and after, as asexual. Coming out as bi was just not a problem. Coming out as ace has been totally different. Maybe most fundamentally, because of the lack of asexual visibility I do almost feel obligated to be a visible ace in a way I never felt when I thought I was bi. Then there's explaining asexuality to hostile queer folx, who're often so deep in the most toxic Tumblr drama and BS that they can't even have a conversation with a real person from outside that warped lens. It's a very poorly understood orientation, and a lot of problems stem from that.

FAA had a similar experience: "I got nothing but positive responses upon coming out as bi, but coming out as trans is a whole different ball game. People were being violent and threatening toward me in school and I wanted nothing more than to leave and start over somewhere else."

Coming Out to Some but Not Others

The majority of participants (33) chose to come out to some people in their lives but not others, generally for safety or comfort reasons. For Cecily, "I'm very openly out to everyone in my new state, but almost no one back home and not at all to my family." Similarly, B declares, "I haven't, nor will I, come out to my parents." And for XA, "I live in a rural community, so I'm not out to anyone except a few family members and some online friends." Q's experience is that "I am still in the process of coming out. My closest friends and significant other know and I wear pride accessories out in public, but my family does not know." Many are very strategic about whom they choose to conceal their identities from. KA, for example, has "only come out to other LGBTQ+ individuals." Similarly, Jack "didn't come out until I had any reason to, and I haven't even explicitly come out to my parents or extended family. If I'm not dating a man, they don't really need to know."

For some, coming out to old friends was more difficult than coming out to new friends. FA's experience is that coming out to my friends was the hardest even though I knew they wouldn't care because there's always that fear of rejection in the back of your mind. It was easier to come out to people I had just met in college because I had less to lose in those friendships. If they rejected me, it wasn't like I would lose an important lifelong friendship as would have been the case with my friends from home. I haven't come out to my family because they are very religious and homophobic.

DAA tells a similar story: "I find it a lot easier to come out to new friends and strangers because they don't have as many preconceived notions. But overall I am still mostly in the closet." Participant O echoes the sentiment: "It's hard to ask the people in your life to look at you differently, I guess. Still haven't told everybody."

Closeted

Eighteen participants reported being closeted at the time of writing. Some plan to come out eventually, while others do not see a need or do not feel safe. Some did come out at one point but went back in the closet for safety reasons. RA cited fear of a damaged reputation: "I would never ever publicly come out if I had a boyfriend while still living in the area, as the full-on gay kids have a reputation as super flamboyant/promiscuous which is not something I want to be umbrellaed under, which is what people would assume, truth or not." Some knew for a fact that their community would be unsupportive. H, for example, is frightened to come out: "I am not able to come out as it is not safe in the town I live in."

For YA, "Coming out to my family isn't probably going to happen for a while. I don't want to have to educate them, I don't want to have the conversation with them mostly because I don't think they will be supportive." IAA was fearful of parental reactions as well: "While my parents are not extremely religious, they still hold their prejudices toward the LGBT community. So much so that it's common in our culture for men to talk about killing their sons if they found out they were gay. They could be accepting of me but I'm not trying to take that chance and waiting until I'm financially independent from them and living at my own place."

Others didn't want the hassle of coming out and having to educate people. For PAA, "In general, my sexuality is not something I talk about to most people, and it never really has been. I am not ashamed of it, but I know that reactions to asexuality can be varied, and that's not really something I need or want to deal with." And for QAA, "My sexuality has come into question among my friends and I have continued to tell that I am straight. I feel as though I am afraid to come out, and I feel apprehensive about the fact that once I am out I will continue to have to come out for the rest of my life." And IA is "not really open about it as my parents very much want me to have a family, and my friends are weird about non-heterosexual people."

Some participants came out and then felt they had to go back in the closet. 'Uhane, for example, "tried coming out once. It didn't go well. I went back into hiding." Others were unsure about when or how to come out. LAA, for example, is "still not really out as not-cis because I am trying to figure out how I want to handle that before I tell most people about it." A few participants did not come out because they were assumed to be queer from a young age. OA recalls, "I never had to make a choice. I was always assumed to be a queer kid by most everyone." One participant, ZA, "never came out directly. I just let people who wanted to figure it out, figure it out." Similarly, Shua "never officially came out. I just treated it like the norm." Another, M, dislikes the term "coming out" because "it situates heterosexuality as the norm. Instead, I invite people in to my queerness as I see fit. My family doesn't know still but I invited in my partner, close friends, and paramours. I do still envy people who had their 'coming out' that was accepted and celebrated. Sometimes I feel that I'm still hiding my identity out of fear and shame."

COMMUNITY REACTIONS

Participants received a variety of community reactions, from positive (kinship with queer community, allyship from friends and peers, and unconditional love from families) to negative (mockery, disbelief, bullying and harassment, physical and sexual violence, and separation from community). Most found support, from families, friends, and partners. Some experienced a distinct lack of support from family and peers, with major themes including bisexual and asexual erasure, statements that "it's just a phase," and intrusive questions.

Supportive Community Members

Thirty-seven participants reported receiving positive community reactions upon coming out, from family (14), friends (18), and partners (5). Peri had supportive parents and friends: "I just sort of mentioned it in high school to someone. Then it was just something that was. My parents just sort of went, 'Okay, now go get ready for work or you'll be late.'" These reactions show that Peri's community was nonchalantly supportive. For Z, some family was immediately supportive while others took a little while to come around: "My mom and dad were always great about it and said they already knew. My mother's family had no issues because my uncle was already gay and out. My dad's family is more southern so a few of them always referred to my girlfriend as my 'friend' but it's gotten better." Q, who is out to close friends, had a mostly supportive coming out: "So far, many have been very accepting and supportive." Perhaps the most wholesome coming out story came from participant AA: "I realized that I still hadn't come out to my brother. As we were talking, a conversation came up about homophobic people and I say, 'Have I told you I'm gay?' knowing full well that I hadn't. He responds with, 'Me too, I'm bi!' and we high fived. Then we talked about our journeys and went along with different conversations."

Unsupportive Community Members

Seventeen participants reported receiving negative community reactions upon coming out, from family (10), peers (6), and colleagues (1). Lane remembers, "The last job I worked in retail, one of my managers laughed at me when I told him about my gender identity. It hurt." Sometimes discouragement came from a place of fear. X's mother "voiced that she wished for me to be straight because being gay was so hard and dangerous in the world. She wished that I could have an easier route through life. The thing is, being gay is even easier than being Black or a woman, and much, much easier than being gay and pretending and forcing myself to be straight." Parents who were initially discouraging sometimes became supportive after accepting their children's gender or sexual identities. Other negative reactions included bullying at school, encouragement from families to conform to heterosexual and cisgender norms, disbelief, bisexual and asexual erasure, statements that it's "just a phase," and intrusive questions and comments.

Bisexual and Asexual Erasure

Both bisexual and asexual participants were subjected to erasure, both from within the LGBTQIA+ community and without. Many bisexuals were accused of "actually" being gay or straight, experimenting, confused, or doing it for attention. Common reactions to bisexual disclosure included "How can you be bisexual if you're dating a woman/man?" and "You're just gay and scared to come out." Sometimes same-sex partners felt fear of being left for an opposite-sex partner, and vice versa. Asexuals were also accused of attention seeking and confusion, and asexuality was called into question as a real and valid identity.

Bisexual participant HAA, for example, "had to come out multiple times to both friends and family because people assumed bisexuality was just a stepping-stone to me coming out as gay or that I would end up with a woman and put that phase behind me. Their assumptions made me question my own identity for years, but ultimately I grew more familiar with my bisexuality and knew it was true for me." FAA recalls, "Even after I came out, people still made me feel like an imposter because I hadn't had sex with a girl, so I couldn't be attracted to one. I hadn't had sex with boys either, but my attraction to them wasn't doubted at all." Some participants experienced internalized erasure. Kate remembers, "I came out as a lesbian when I was fourteen or fifteen, and then I started feeling attracted to men a couple years later, which was super weird. I came out as bi when I was around eighteen, and I felt like I was letting the team down. (I still feel like I let the team down)."

"It's Just a Phase"

The majority of folks who came out before or around adolescence received some pushback that their gender or sexual identity was "just a phase." Lesbians were told by men, "I can change that." Asexuals were told, "You just haven't found the right person yet."[9] Asexuals were also accused of having hormone problems or told that they were late bloomers. Most younger participants were told, "You're too young to know."

Sometimes intercommunity hostility occurred. For Rose, "coming out was probably one of the most freeing and yet negative experiences of my life. The lesbians around me wanted me to be a lesbian and told me that my bisexuality was just a phase on that road." EA delayed coming out because of reactions like this. "I didn't come out until last year because there is a lot of hate toward bisexual people. People think we're promiscuous and that we're just going through a phase. Or that we're gay, and not yet ready to come out." F also delayed coming out, for the same reasons: "I came out slowly, later, when I was in college. It took a long time for me to accept my sexuality. It felt like no one trusted what I knew about my sexuality (i.e., 'phases/experimentation') until I was an adult."

Intrusive Questions

Several participants experienced intrusive questions and statements about their sexual or gender identities. Asexuals, being one of the most poorly understood orientations, received the brunt of this. Common questions included: "Do you masturbate?" "Have you ever had sex?" "How do you know you're asexual if you've never tried sex?" "Were you raped as a child?" "Do you have erectile dysfunction?" "What's the point of dating if you're not going to have sex?" and "Are you sure you're not just a lesbian/gay?" They were also subjected to countless jokes about plants being asexual.[10] Participant IA recalls, "I came out to my two closest friends, and nobody else yet. They weren't really surprised, but they asked a couple intrusive questions and statements. 'Does everything work okay?' 'You just don't want children,' 'Are you sure?' are the notable ones." And for CA, "The worst I experienced coming out was intrusive questions about masturbation. I have heard a number of casual bigoted comments from people who I am not out to, and it has been a barrier to coming out for a while."

9

TRANSITION

Thirty-three transgender participants in this study reported undertaking some form of gender transition to better align their presentation, legal status, and/or physical bodies with their felt genders. Transition was a fraught topic: For many trans participants, details were too intimate and private to want to share in great detail. However, several participants generously shared their experiences with social, legal, and medical/surgical transition. Not all transgender participants transitioned. Some trans participants could not transition due to various barriers, and some trans participants chose not to transition for a variety of reasons.

TIMING

Very few participants transitioned before the age of eighteen. Reasons cited were lack of access to transition-related resources or not yet having come to a realization about their gender identity. Most participants transitioned between ages eighteen and thirty. Some waited until after thirty, mostly for logistical and safety reasons. Earlier cohorts who started transition later in life often had major challenges with presentation and passing. Because they had been practicing the assigned gender behaviors, grooming, and speech patterns for so long, it was difficult to learn the behaviors of the affirmed gender: "Because of secrecy, many transsexual and transgender people are forced to learn gender behaviors belonging to an incongruent gender behavior category. They spend less time practicing the gender behaviors belonging to their congruent gender behavior category. Consequently when transsexuals and transgender people come out, they have much remedial learning to do to be perceived as authentic."[1]

Early: Before Age Eighteen

Only two transgender participants in this study began their gender transitions before the age of eighteen. Both of them began in high school, with social transition. They dressed, groomed, and presented as their true genders and requested new names and personal gender pronouns. Neither of them began legal or medical/surgical transition elements until after the age of eighteen. Lane began social transition in high school and is currently pursuing surgical options: "I chose not to go on hormones. I have an appointment with a surgeon to get double incision with nipple graft."

Mid: Age Eighteen to Age Thirty

The majority (16) of participants began their transitions between the ages of eighteen and thirty. Like the younger participants, most of them began with social transition before pursuing medical or surgical options or obtaining legal name or sex changes. Medical transition or "second puberty" sometimes felt awkward and uncomfortable for older participants. For Christina, "the fact that my body is older than my perceived age causes a type of mental dissonance."

Late: After Age Thirty

Nine participants reported beginning their transitions after the age of thirty. Most of them didn't previously have access to transition options due to financial hardship, societal transphobia and closeting, and/or job and housing instability. Two participants came to realize their gender identities when they were in their early thirties. Seren, for example, began to transition right away, as finances permitted: "I'm transitioning as much as I can afford. And I've already taken care of most of the legal process. As soon as I learned things about myself, I took whatever steps I could, and could afford to, to transition pretty much as soon as I made the decisions."

PROCESS

Transition is a process with several possible elements: social, legal, and medical/surgical.[2] Most transgender people—twenty-four in this study—pick and choose what elements to pursue. Those who take a more traditional path are often encouraged to do so by gatekeeping medical professionals.[3] However, many purposely choose a traditional path to combat dysphoria and to pass as cisgender.

Social Transition

Social transition involves making changes in how one presents oneself to others. Many transgender people change their names and personal gender pronouns. Trans women and AMAB nonbinary people may make other changes, such as wearing more feminine clothing; removing body and/or facial hair; using breast, hip, or buttock prostheses; or tucking. Tucking involves slipping the testes into the inguinal canals and holding them in place with tight underwear or a garment called a gaff, which may be homemade using nylon stockings.

Trans men and AFAB nonbinary people may make other changes, such as wearing more masculine clothing, growing out body hair, binding (compressing chest tissue using sports bras, Ace bandages,[4] or a compression vest called a binder), or packing (using a penile prosthesis). It must be stressed that this is not a complete list of possible social transition elements, nor is it a roadmap to be followed completely. Rather, most trans people choose some but not others. Some stop here and others go on to pursue legal and/or medical/surgical transition.

Joe is one participant who experienced a complex social transition as well as a very helpful medical intervention:

> My transitioning as a genderqueer individual has been a seemingly low-effort affair, but has meant a lot for my own well-being. The first part of my transition was stopping my periods through the use of a

hormonal IUD. I also started going by my nickname more, Joe, which I acquired in middle school when a group of girl friends and I decided to go by traditionally "boy" names for a day and mine was just fitting. I also started using they/them pronouns, which has been really validating being around people who use that instead of she/her. I also wear more men's clothing because that is what I am most comfortable in, but have a few dresses when I'm in the mood. Lastly, I stopped stressing so much about body expectations and shave very little body hair anymore.

Legal Transition

Legal transition involves changing one's legal documents to reflect one's true gender. This can mean legally changing one's name and/or obtaining an official change of gender in court. Changing legal sex is often a necessary requirement to accessing medical and surgical transition care, as well as changing other legal and financial documents such as driver's license, social security card, passport, birth certificate, lease and mortgage documents, medical records, credit cards, bank accounts, and so forth. In some states and jurisdictions, one can change these documents without a legal change of sex, but a legal name change is always needed for changing names on official documents.

Again, some transgender people stop after obtaining their legal name and/or gender changes, while others pursue medical and/or surgical transition. Actually, legally changing one's name and gender and obtaining new personal records and documents can be so frustrating, time-consuming, and expensive that many transgender people either do not pursue these options at all or make attempts but ultimately fail to achieve legal recognition. Furthermore, some identification documents, such as US passports and most US states' birth certificates, do not allow a third-gender designation, presenting yet another hurdle for nonbinary people seeking legal recognition.

Medical/Surgical Transition

Medical/surgical transition involves medication, therapies, and surgeries to physically align the physical body with one's true gender. For trans women and AMAB nonbinary people, this can include hormone replacement therapy (typically estrogen and a testosterone blocker) to develop breast tissue, soften the skin, and reduce body hair. Other interventions include voice therapy, fertility preservation, permanent hair removal through electrolysis or laser treatment, breast augmentation surgery, facial feminization surgeries (which make the facial features smaller), orchiectomy, and vaginoplasty.

For trans men and AFAB nonbinary people, medical/surgical transition can include hormone replacement therapy (testosterone) in order to develop facial and body hair, muscle mass, and clitoral tissue. Other interventions include voice therapy, fertility preservation, mastectomy and chest reshaping, hysterectomy, metoidioplasty, and phalloplasty.

For youth who have affirming medical providers and accepting parents or guardians, puberty-suppressing medications are an option. Again, it's important to note that people pick and choose which medical/surgical elements, if any, to pursue. It's equally important to keep in mind that choice is often constrained by economic and accessibility factors, as well as gatekeeping within the medical industry.

PA followed a traditional path to transfeminine transition: "I have transitioned all the way, legally, socially, medically including GCS/SRS.[5] HRT brought about Puberty 2.0 and luckily living in the NYC area, there are a lot of resources here. My second puberty was less awkward and it was wonderful to experience my body aligning with my brain." So far, Seren has been in medical transition through hormone replacement therapy: "Second puberty has been amazing. My body and mind began to feel so much more at ease as I decreased my testosterone, and I felt so much more like myself as I started estrogen."

EXPERIENCES

While most participants felt good about their transitions and experienced happiness and gender euphoria, some found the process frustrating. Some participants experienced gatekeeping and were not able to access affirming care. Others were forced into a traditional path when they really wanted to pick and choose transition elements. And some found that the experience was physically painful or had unanticipated and unwanted side effects. Finally, some trans participants chose not to transition.

Exciting

The majority of participants had a mostly positive experience with their transition. They used words like "amazing," "exciting," "enjoyable," and "life-saving." For Tommie Jayne, "the main thing that changed for me was not being self-conscious about how I moved, posed or spoke and being made for a queer. I could finally be queer out loud and didn't have to play dude anymore." HA is "starting to use they/them pronouns at home and work. I am thinking of getting a binder and have started dressing more gender neutrally on the weekend. It is a scary but exciting process." And for W, "being able to transition saved my life."

Erin has also had a mostly positive transition: "I began going to gender therapy when I was thirty-five and got right on estradiol and T-blockers. I legally changed my name and gender marker. With the HRT I have noticed a decrease in energy and strength, my skin has gotten softer and emotionally I feel more balanced." This sense of balance was echoed by many participants on hormone replacement therapy; the correct hormones can bring about a sense of personal ease with one's body and mind.

Christina is mostly excited about her transition but knows that parts of it will be challenging:

> I'm very aware of the changes in my body, as opposed to my first puberty where I was more aware of the external world. The fact that I'm feeling some emotional relief through HRT is making puberty seem awesome, so far. I know my body needs to go through changes, and I know it's going to be rough sometimes, so I'm able to get through the painful parts and appreciate the wonderful easier parts.

NAA was also cognizant of difficulties while still enjoying transition: "Overall, being able to live openly as nonbinary feels like a huge burden off of my shoulders. It can be frustrating to be so visible, to have to educate people, but it's still better than constantly pretending to be something I'm not."

LA compares medical transition to first puberty: "Since going on testosterone, I've gotten a bunch of new things to be excited about. Medical transition is just everything I wanted out of first puberty before my body screwed me over." Y experienced gender euphoria midway through transition: "My favorite memory was that I never looked in a full body mirror until fairly late into hormones. The first time I did I only saw the chest and below. I honestly thought it was someone else and thought she was gorgeous. Then I realized it was me and got very happy."

Frustrating

Seven participants in the study experienced frustration or other emotional pain during their transition, including one who was gatekept from affirming medical interventions. They used words like "depressing," "difficult," "frustrating," and "painful." For T, "it was depressing at times looking back to realize I had no one to share these changes with or talk to about what I was going through. It has been very difficult; very little support from anyone and having to navigate it on my own." Social isolation and loneliness were common for transgender participants, particularly those in earlier cohorts. 'Uhane had a very challenging medical transition: "I had 'second puberty' when I started on testosterone after my intersex diagnosis. It was difficult. I wasn't in a society of boys all going through the same thing, I was in a society of very fucking serious grad students who didn't have time or bandwidth for my bullshit."

For participants in earlier cohorts who transitioned later in life, age was a significant factor in their negative experiences. Anni relates, "Second puberty is more frustrating because I'm thirty-five now, and only three years into medical transition." The effects of hormone replacement therapy are better the younger a patient starts. For older patients, they may have fully developed breasts or hair loss that make hormone replacement therapy far less helpful. As mentioned above, puberty-suppressing medications are available for prepubescent and pubescent youth. They arrest puberty so that, upon the age of majority, the youth can decide which hormone option they desire and either go off the meds, having a natural puberty, or begin hormone replacement therapy. However, none of the participants in this study had this option available to them.

Choosing Not to Transition

Fifteen transgender participants have not transitioned, either because they do not wish to (4), because they are unsure what they want to pursue (9), due to gatekeeping (1), or due to disability interfering with transition (1). Participant B has a spouse who is not currently okay with testosterone therapy: "Eventually I will start HRT. I just need my spouse to get comfortable with the idea. I've waited this long, I can wait some more. I sometimes dream of menopause." Several participants have not started transition because they don't know what they want yet. MA, for example, would "like to try low-dose T maybe but also maybe not." LAA is "currently seeking therapy to help me figure out what I should do about next steps. I am still not sure what I want."

One participant, K, is unable to pursue transition options due to disability: "I want to wear a chest binder—it would help with the dysphoria—but I have a chronic condition that would interfere. I haven't really had the energy to do anything significant that would identify me as trans." Finally, one participant has been blocked from medical transition by medical personnel. P has "been trying to start testosterone since high school, but I'm being kept from it to this day 'for my mental health.'"

10

WHAT WE WISH HAD BEEN DIFFERENT

In this study, the final question of the survey was: "What do you wish had been different?" The responses were numerous, thoughtful, insightful, and heartbreaking. Participants talked about how they wished they had been accepted by family and friends. They wished for less intercommunity hostility and less stigma and discrimination in the wider community. Participants also wrote extensively about resources they wished they had had access to as youth, as well as particular experiences they wished had been different. In this chapter, we learn from the wisdom of participants as they muse about their ideal adolescences. Finally, we finish with a concrete action plan for parents, school staff, and clinicians to better support the LGBTQIA+ youth in their lives.

ACCEPTANCE

Sixty-eight participants spoke movingly about their desire for acceptance from family, friends, the queer community, and the wider community. Specifically, they wished for less stigma, less bullying, less abuse, greater access to affirming healthcare, and the ability to have explored their genders and/or sexualities during their adolescence. Simply being witnessed and seeing oneself mirrored in another's eyes can be intensely affirming as well.[1]

Family and Friends

Thirty-one participants wrote extensively about how acceptance and support from family and friends would have significantly improved their adolescence experiences. OAA put it succinctly: "I wish my parents weren't homophobic and transphobic." For DAA, "Ideally I would have wanted my parents to express more acceptance about LGBT issues. I am still unsure and they are fairly conservative so I'm not out to them." In the absence of stated support, many queer youth will keep their identity secret, not sharing a vital part of their identity with the people who are supposed to know them best. FA spoke passionately about the burden of secrecy. "I wish people in my life had been more vocal about supporting the LGBTQ community. I would've felt more safe knowing there were people who supported me. My ideal adolescence would have been one where I didn't have to hide a huge part of my identity. It gets exhausting having to pretend to be something you're not for that long."

Seven participants experienced physical and/or sexual abuse in their youth and wished that they had not undergone those experiences. For Zoe, "Childhood trauma affected my ability to learn and be engaged in my classes, so I wish I hadn't had so much trauma so I could have learned more." Trauma can affect the physical body, mental and cognitive functioning, and emotional regulation. Learning is impacted, as is biological development in general.[2] Particularly if the trauma was caused by identity-based abuse, personal and social identity can be significantly impaired.

Two participants wished that they had had access to mental health therapy as adolescents. For ZA, "I wish my family was more open to the idea of professional help so I could have gone somewhere when I was confused about things sexually." K had access to therapy for a short while, but wished for more: "If I'd been able to see a therapist for a longer period of time, I think I would be more comfortable with my own identity."

Twelve participants wished that their parents had supported them in exploring their genders and/or sexualities as adolescents. One participant, Lane, articulated that their ideal adolescence would have included a supportive family that encouraged identity exploration: "I wish my dad was more accepting and wanted to help me be my true self."

Skylar echoed this sentiment: "I would have just liked more support and options. More openness and ability to explore things about myself without fear of judgment or prejudice." For Christina, supportive parents and community would have made a significant positive impact on her adolescence. She also wished for "honesty about sex and gender, and less stigma" from her family. Maddie also had thoughts about this: "I wish that my parents knew to expect that I'd be gay. I wish they'd exposed me to more queer people and queer media, and really enforced gay positivity with me and my sister."

Intercommunity

One participant wrote poignantly about intercommunity hostility. Identity-based cliques form and prejudices can fester. For example, a very vocal minority of cisgender lesbians identify as trans-exclusionary radical feminists (TERFs) and vociferously dismiss transgender experiences and exclude transgender women from women's spaces. As previously discussed, bisexuals and asexuals are sometimes excluded from queer community and their identities picked over, excluded, and discriminated against. Lateral violence is also enacted upon femme-presenting people,[3] as well as on QTBIPOC[4] by white queers.

Additionally, there is vitriol within the transgender community: Transmedicalists[5] believe that transgender people must all experience dysphoria and pursue medical transition, minimizing the experiences and validity of transgender people who do not experience dysphoria or who do not wish to undergo medical or surgical transition. There is also hostility between older generations who prefer the term "transsexual" and younger generations who find that term outdated and medicalized, as well as hostility between binary trans people who do not believe that nonbinary people fit under the transgender umbrella and nonbinary people who believe that they do.

Unfortunately, intercommunity hostility distracts us from the real threats: patriarchy, white supremacy, homophobia, and transphobia from the wider society.

Wider Community

Twenty-four participants discussed stigma and discrimination from the wider community. Negative popular views and portrayals of LGBTQIA+ people abound. Transgender women are inaccurately cast as "men in dresses," gay men are demonized as promiscuous, and lesbians are said to be fat and ugly. This is only the tip of the iceberg. Queer people hear awful things about themselves on a regular basis, from jokes on television to discriminatory bills based on gender stereotypes and fears. Participants talked about how damaging and stigmatizing negative stereotypes were for them, both as adolescents and now as adults. BAA pointed out that "growing up, most movies, TV shows and comedy specials made queer people out to be weirdos who basically live on a different planet. Maybe me and other people I know would have been able to live their truth sooner."

W made a connection between societal intolerance and self-esteem: "I wish I could have grown up in an environment that didn't teach me to hate myself for being different." Isaako was not optimistic about societal acceptance, stating that "freaks like me will never be welcome by society. We challenge and threaten everything they stand for. The best I can hope for is that someday society will mature enough to accept *all* its people, and that every child can grow up to be healthy, happy and productive, like me."

RESOURCES

More than two-thirds of participants (103) spoke about how they wished they had better resources as adolescents. Specifically, people talked about how better sexuality education would have significantly improved their adolescence experiences. They also wished for more and better books and other media, as well as queer-affirming programs and safe spaces to be themselves.

School Curricula

Forty-five participants had extensive suggestions for improving the school curriculum. They wished for LGBTQIA+ representation in sexuality education, as well as better and more accurate sex ed in general.[6] They also wished for representation in the wider curriculum, particularly history. Many people had suggestions for improving sexual education. For Joe, "My ideal adolescence would have first included a sexual education that involved human anatomy, safe sex practices, queer terminology, the importance of consent, and gender exploration. On top of that, it would have included people around me creating a safe place for me to open up about my sexuality and gender sooner." CJ also criticized sexual education: "It should be taught earlier and include much more including gender and sexuality spectrums and by people who know what they're talking about." Erin also wished for information about sexuality and gender identity in school: "I think if I had an understanding of what I was feeling that it would have possibly helped me come to the realization of who I am."

Shua complained about the "blatant lack of any talk of sexuality. There is also the gendering of genitals that I've always hated." Skylar also had some thoughts about language: "It would also be good if the language was 'people with uteruses' and 'people with penises.'" Affirming language like that includes transgender people without misgendering them. Skylar also would have liked if, in high school, "we had talked about queer content in a way that wasn't inherently political." They also articulated that sex ed should not be a single-day topic but should be taught in multiple lessons.

X wanted queer inclusion in sex education classes: "Have material in media or lesson plans or just a general acknowledgment that not all children are straight." Nora echoed this: "Teachers could have explicitly mentioned queer people in sex ed—I was not the only gay or trans person at my school and I know it would have helped us all tremendously." It is vital for youth to see themselves represented in lesson plans; youth who are marginalized in this way are made invisible and often feel as if their identities are somehow wrong or bad. Furthermore, there are health risks specific to LGBTQIA+ populations[7] that should be discussed in high school health classes. IAA is studying to work in healthcare and "just realized that there is healthcare information specific to the LGBT community. It's super dangerous to not have that information available to adolescent kids, whether they're LGBT or even questioning their identity."

Some people had sex education that included some queer identities but not others. It was very common, for example, for asexual identities to be unrepresented. Aly did not learn about asexual identities until well after school for this reason: "I wish someone had mentioned that it was okay to not like anyone. All the messaging was focused on 'it's okay to like whoever you like' and since everyone else seemed to like someone, I sometimes felt like there was something wrong with me." CAA was another participant who did not learn about asexual identities in school: "I wish I'd known about asexuality as a full sexuality earlier—I kind of knew it was a thing people could be, but had no concept of it as a queer identity. Good, inclusive sex ed certainly could have helped with that."

In addition to hoping for queer inclusion, participants also widely disparaged abstinence-only curricula. M, for example, stated,

> I wish there was LGBTQ+ inclusive and sex-positive sexual educa-
> tion. The abstinence-only model failed the majority of my peers,
> myself included. There was no talk about gender identity/expression,
> sexual orientation, relationship structures outside monogamy, or oth-
> er sexual practices (BDSM/kink). This would have shaped my devel-
> opment in a positive way rather than dealing with years of shame,
> guilt, fear, isolation, and confusion.

Doing away with the abstinence-only model would also allow for discussions of safer sex in a realistic and practical way. When youth don't know how to prevent pregnancy and STI transmission, pregnancies and STIs happen. Zoe wished for "way better more comprehensive sex education from an actual sex educator. I wish we had covered gender identity and different forms of protection."

Seren thought that sex education should be greatly expanded to talk about important sexuality topics: "Sex ed should be 'sex' ed. There could have been stuff about consent, and negotiating pleasure, and actual facts instead of scare tactics, and resources." QA wished "I had a broader understanding of sex and all its manifestations, identities, less repression and more exploration, and just more acceptance of others in general." Rose urged "practical, accurate information about gender and sexuality, and a supportive community not bent on education, marriage, and children as the 'normal' life path." Positioning one type of lifestyle (a typical heterosexual middle-to-upper-class path, at that) leaves out the diversity of life choices and identities, including working in the trades or military, polyamory, asexuality, and being childfree whether by choice or by circumstance. Rather than privileging one (already privileged) life path, Rose wished that all life choices and identities were portrayed positively.

Participants also hoped for queer representation in the wider curricula beyond sex education. YA stated, "I wish gender and sexual orientation was discussed in school. I wish we were taught LGBTQIA+ history." And Q said, "I wish my teachers had mentioned the existence of LGBT+ people. We were essentially never talked about." Lane thought that history curricula in particular should include queer history topics: "I wish teachers would incorporate LGBT topics into the curriculum. It would be nice if there was more representation in history, for example." It is crucial for youth to know their history. Without queer inclusion, students may not learn about queer political history, laws and bills affecting queer communities, queer activists and politicians, and queer culture. Without this knowledge youth may believe that they have no history or culture.

And beyond helping students gain knowledge and self-confidence about their identities, inclusive curricula make school a safer and more productive place for queer students. According to a GLSEN research brief, LGBTQIA+ students in schools with inclusive curricula were less likely to experience sexuality- and gender-based victimization, less likely to feel unsafe at school, and less likely to miss school due to feeling unsafe.[8] Furthermore, in schools with inclusive curricula, cisgender and heterosexual students were more likely to accept and respect LGBTQIA+ students.[9] Students were less likely to use or hear homophobic slurs and negative comments about gender expression and more likely to intervene when hearing these comments. Inclusive curricula are good for all students, promote tolerance and empathy, make schools safer for all, and provide evidence-based teachings.

Books and Other Media

Fifty-one participants lacked books and other media that provided positive representations of LGBTQIA+ people. People wished for queer portrayals in young adult and juvenile fiction, "own voices" representation, more and better nonfiction, and representation for the less visible identities such as asexuality, bisexuality, and nonbinary identities.

Once again, Joe had some terrific concrete suggestions for resources:

> More resources available to youth at earlier ages. There are age-appropriate books or pamphlets that can be created to cover from grades K–12 and made available in public libraries and schools. For really young kids, simply having queer relationships in texts would be a good start. Preteens and teens need texts with more vocabulary and characters struggling with or creating a sexual or gender identity. Due to some youths having to worry about family or caretakers' mistreatment if they were caught reading anything queer related, texts could have vague or obscure titles to reduce the chances of harm.

Others had more specific needs. Several bisexual and asexual participants wished that there were more resources focused on these identities, as they are less visible. HAA said, "I wish I had known about bisexuality and seen it represented in media more. Knowing it was an option might have helped me figure out my identity sooner." Similarly, Cecily "would've loved to know more about bisexuality so I wouldn't have been confused and ashamed for so many years."

RK wrote poignantly about "own voices" representation: in other words, media about marginalized identities created by people who share those identities. In particular, he noted that academic research about asexuality is often performed by allosexual, or non-asexual, researchers. Some of this research is viewed as deeply flawed by folks in the asexual community:

> There are several books that have been written about the ace spectrum, some of them by asexuals and some by researchers. I don't know of any written by an ace and a researcher and that would be really great. There was a whole kerfuffle on Tumblr about the researcher who came up with the term for someone who experiences sexual arousal and libido and a desire to participate in that but does not imagine themselves in a sexual scenario—autochorrisexuality—and he describes it as a paraphilia. People took issue with him describing it as a paraphilia, so they came up with their own term, aegosexuality. Stuff like that could be avoided if the ace community worked with researchers.

Programs and Safe Spaces

Safe spaces are places where LGBTQIA+ youth feel physically and emotionally safe, affirmed, and celebrated. Some are queer-specific spaces, such as queer centers, support groups, queer events, and so forth. But a classroom with a mix of students can be a safe space as well if the teacher is willing to acknowledge, protect, and respect the queer and trans youth in their classroom.[10] In a 2005 study of middle school students, researcher Samantha Chandler made some cogent suggestions for how to create a safer classroom. Suggestions included being an advocate for all students through resources, programs, bullying intervention, acknowledging that queerness exists in everyday life and throughout history, and queer teachers being out.[11]

Seven participants spoke about how queer-affirming programs and safe spaces would have impacted their adolescence experiences. They wished for LGBTQIA+ centers in their areas, anti-bullying measures in their schools, and that their libraries were safer spaces for them. Lane would have appreciated it "if there were posters for hotlines and information websites in libraries and resource centers." They mused further about safe spaces: "I wish there were more LGBT centers in my area. I also wish libraries could be safe spaces." Many public libraries strive to be safe spaces for marginalized patrons. Some libraries, however, do not make all their patrons feel safe. Some participants linked safe spaces to mental health. HA articulated that "I think I would have had less issues with depression and suicidal ideation if I had had a safe space and opportunity to learn about sexual orientation and gender."

Social media was seen as a safe space for some participants. There are many online communities (including subreddits, Tumblr pages, Facebook groups, forums, and so forth) created by and for the queer community and more granular communities within.[12] Some participants wished that social media had been available in their youth so they could have built community in that way. 'Uhane, for example, wished "that I'd been born thirty years later. I really could have used social media wherein I could participate anonymously in large-population forums to figure things out. As it is, I have very few people to talk to about these things."

EXPERIENCES

Many participants wrote about particular experiences they wished had been different in their adolescence. Common topics included wishing for better and more role models and allies, earlier self-knowledge and coming out, and earlier or different transitions.

Role Models and Allies

Thirty-three participants wished they had had better and more role models and allies. It is important for LGBTQIA+ folks, especially youth, to have queer role models. Visibility normalizes queerness, decreases societal stigma, and makes youth safer. Allies are vital as well. Participants spoke about how queer-affirming teachers and doctors in particular would have been positive for them in both youth and adulthood.

Participant I spoke eloquently about how queer models would have significantly improved their adolescence:

> I wish I had been surrounded by queer people of different racial, ethnic, and class backgrounds in every area of my life and seen a lot of different models for what a queer life could look like. I wish that conversations about gender and sexuality had been proactive and invited me to ask questions of myself and others from a much younger age. I wish conversations about gender and sexuality had been more linked to conversations about race, ethnicity, power, and privilege.

Role models can be as simple as peers who are out. For Joe, "The thing I wish most was different when I was an adolescent was that I wish I could have known someone like me. If there had been someone who I could have confided in about my feelings regarding gender and sexuality and would have let me know it was okay to explore that side of myself, maybe things would have been different." Similarly, Peri stated that "more visibility of these communities would have been helpful. For a long time, I didn't even know they were out there. It was just gay/ straight in my world. Being able to see people like me would have made me feel more secure in a time of my life when I felt the most insecure."

Participants also hoped for allies. Several mentioned that having teachers who were out themselves or allies for queer youth would have been a positive addition to their adolescence experiences. After Maddie graduated from high school, "I learned that like every single good teacher I'd ever had was a lesbian—I know teachers don't owe students information about their personal lives, but it would have really helped me to know that my favorite English and art teachers were married, and that five of my other favorite teachers were lesbians married to other women. My negative stereotypes about lesbians would have been shattered way earlier."

WA had a specific suggestion. They wished that "someone in authority in my community telling us it was okay and normal to be LGBT+. They should have actively been nipping the 'that's gay' trend." Youth using the word "gay" as an insult is quite common, and it is hurtful for gay students. Jack also spoke about the importance of allyship: "Parents, teachers, and school counselors need to make it obvious that they are allies and have some lifeline to help people struggling with identity."

Several participants spoke about the importance of healthcare providers being affirming, educated, and competent allies. T suggested that "mental and medical health providers should do their own research and/or attend conferences, reach out to learn from other trans people or allies that advocate for trans people and provide education. Clients/patients should not be responsible for educating." Nora had a particularly bad experience with a doctor as an adolescent: "My pediatrician was just awful about it. As soon as I came out to her at what was supposed to be my first Pap/gynecological exam, she immediately said we didn't have to do it because I wasn't at risk for anything (didn't know gay women couldn't get cervical cancer but okay)."

Self-Knowledge and Coming Out

Twenty-six participants wished that they had known sooner about their genders and/or sexualities. Four wished that they had done more sexual experimentation earlier to figure things out. Several participants, the majority of whom were transgender, wished that they had come out earlier. C would have liked "access to information. Had I known definitions of trans when I was younger, I would have transitioned a very long time ago." Similarly, Kae wished "I had known about trans people when

I was a child. I definitely would have identified as a trans boy if I had known what that meant back then."

Anni wished "I'd have come out when I first realized I was trans. I could have avoided most of the facial hair." Maddie said, "I wish I'd come out earlier. It would have saved me a lot of trouble." Z echoes that sentiment: "I wish I could have been out so I would have gotten the chance to date like most teens. I feel like I missed out on a lot of those teenage milestones while being in the closet." A few participants articulated that they wished they had done more sexual experimenting as adolescents so they could have figured out their sexualities earlier. RA, for example, wished "I had experimented more. I would've loved to find out sooner about my bisexuality."

Transition

Ten transgender participants wished that they had been able to transition earlier. They specifically wished that they had had access to puberty blockers in childhood. Seren articulated that she wished she could have transitioned in her early youth:

> I wish I could have been exposed to ideas about gender and sexuality at a much younger age. I wish I could've transitioned earlier in life before testosterone made so many permanent changes to my body. The ideal adolescence would have been starting HRT at first puberty, and living my life as a young woman in my teenage years. Even more ideal would have been living my whole life that way, so I could have spent the kind of time with my mother that she spent with my sister.

T also wished for earlier exposure to information and self-knowledge: "I wish someone knew what was going on with me. I wish I could have transitioned sooner. It would have saved me so much distress."

FAA echoed this wish: "I wish I could have come out sooner and transitioned as a kid to not have to jump through so many hoops now. My ideal adolescence would have been me living my life as a boy and getting my mental health taken care of years earlier." For Y, "Ideally I would have had the right environment to come out way earlier and start at a way better time with hormones." NAA had the same wish: "Ideally I would have been taught from a young age that trans people existed. I would have never been told that my very existence is unnatural or a sin. I would have felt safe expressing my feelings about my gender to my parents. I would have been able to get on puberty blockers and eventually HRT before the damage of female puberty was done."

P also wished for puberty blockers. "I wish I had known I was trans by like age eight so I could have been put on puberty blockers. I could have legally changed my name as a minor. I wouldn't have to have top surgery." And V "would have liked to have been educated about trans issues, that HRT was a thing, etc. before becoming an adult and passing an age when medical transitioning produces the best results. I have a lot of regret and anger that it took me so long to realize my identity and what could be done to make me feel better."

Other Experiences

Some participants had very specific experiences that they wished had been different. Seven wished that they had not been raised in religious households because their families' religions were oppressive to LGBTQIA+ people. One participant wished that they had been raised neutrally. And one queer, trans, intersex participant wished that he had been born heterosexual, cisgender, and dyadic to avoid the pain his identities bring him.

Five participants expressed both happiness for and jealousy of younger queer and trans folks, saying that they wish they had been born later in order to have a better experience. Tommie Jayne, for example, "would love to have had what I see trans kids experiencing now. My life would have been completely different if I had been raised like Kim Petras or Jazz Jennings." B had a similar response: "I look at these young kids transitioning at this young age with the acceptance of their peers, and even their families . . . and I'm so *happy* for them. I wish we had that."

Several participants spoke about how religion negatively impacted them as adolescents due to oppressive and patriarchal language that affected how their families and communities accepted them as well as how they accepted their own identities and behaviors. Ellie, for example, wished that "I hadn't been steered in wayward or confusing directions by a false religion. I was brainwashed by a cult that puts high standards on their boys and girls alike. I was often wallowing in guilt and sadness as a youth because I shamed myself for masturbating or performing a sexually 'deviant' act with another person." For O, "just knowing that queerness existed as something other than the twisted sexual deviancy that religious communities see it as would have changed everything."

G also grew up with a religious upbringing: "I wish my adolescence hadn't been so wrapped up in the Christian religion so that peers and even teachers would bully me for being different. If teachers would have just stopped the other kids from bullying me, that would have made a world of difference. The traditional Christian attitude is very damaging for anyone who isn't cisgender or heteronormative."

Several participants had very specific wishes for their adolescences and ongoing lives. MA spoke about the frustrations of not having the right language for or societal understanding of gender: "I wish gender was further along the process of falling apart a lot sooner. I'm still waiting for the words to talk about mine." OA had a specific support need: "I wish I was told that I was deserving of a partner who would not expect me to be more gender normal." Lane wished they had been raised more neutrally. Several participants mentioned bathroom access, both access to gendered bathrooms for binary transgender people and access to gender neutral restrooms for nonbinary, questioning, or closeted people. And 'Uhane would have liked to wish away his situation altogether.

ACTION PLAN

There are many things that we can do to better support our queer and trans youth. Participants in this study offered a large number of excellent suggestions that have data to back them up. In this section, I share some concrete actions that parents, school staff, and clinicians can take in order to support, affirm, keep safe, and treat the queer youth in their lives. Please note that this is not an exhaustive list but rather a small sample of suggestions. I recommend using this as a jumping-off point and speaking with other queer people and organizations to discover local needs.

For Parents

Support and Acceptance

Unconditional support and acceptance are vital for your queer youth to thrive. This includes believing your child when they tell you who they are, keeping their personal information safe, advocating for them, and helping them explore their identities. Concretely, this can look like:

- Talking about queer politics, current events, and culture in a positive way, whether or not your child is LGBTQIA+ (or out yet).
- Providing informational and entertainment resources that represent queer and trans identities.
- Providing accurate and frank sexual education to fill in gaps in school curricula.
- Making a deliberate effort not to enforce gender-based restrictions (like not allowing a perceived boy to wear a dress, or not allowing a perceived girl to play sports).
- Responding to a child's coming out with love and acceptance.[13]
- Using your child's preferred name and pronouns, even when they're not with you at the moment.
- Not outing your child to others without their permission.
- Advocating for your child to use their preferred restroom in their school.
- Advocating for Safe Zone and other trainings for school personnel.
- And more! Ask your child or queer friends for more thoughts on how to best support your child.

Resources and Treatments

Making resources and necessary treatments accessible for your child is also crucial. Resources include informational, educational, and entertainment media with queer representation. Treatments include mental health therapy and gender affirming therapy and treatment. For your family, this might look like:

- Educating yourself about your child's gender or sexual identity, as well as the full spectrum of queer and trans identities.

- Providing age-appropriate books and other resources, both fiction and nonfiction.
- Advocating for your child's school to include LGBTQIA+ resources and inclusion in the curriculum.
- Educating yourself about puberty blockers and offering them as an option to your transgender child. Whatever you do, please do not attempt conversion therapy.[14]
- Supporting your child in their coming out and social transition.
- And more! Ask your local librarian for current resources for yourself or to share with your child. If your child is transgender, check out the World Professional Association for Transgender Health (WPATH) for up-to-date standards of care.[15]

For School Staff

Curriculum

It is absolutely vital to include LGBTQIA+ identities in the curriculum, both in health/sex education classes and in the broader curriculum.[16] More specific guidelines include the following:

- Making sex education more comprehensive by including information about safer sex practices for all genital configurations and sexual behaviors, discussing issues of consent and sexual pleasure, and avoiding abstinence-only scare tactics.[17]
- Making sex education more inclusive by talking about queer and trans identities, including the less visible ones, discussing health-care disparities and specific population risks, using neutral non-gendered language to refer to body parts, and including information about different relationship structures and other sexual practices such as polyamory and kink.[18]
- Including LGBTQIA+ topics in the broader curriculum. Consider talking about Keith Haring in art class, Sylvia Rivera in history class, and Leslie Feinberg in English class. Talk to your local librarian or queer educator for more ideas.

Restrooms, Pronouns, and Preferred Names

Students need to be able to express themselves as their true selves, including having their names and pronouns respected and being able to use the bathroom appropriate to their needs. To support your students in these ways, consider the following:

- Asking for preferred names and pronouns at the beginning of each class. Be sure to use private notecards and have students specify if they want you to use their name and/or pronouns in the classroom or around their parents or guardians.
- Including an element for preferred name in school record systems. Additionally, make it easy for students to change their gender marker in their school records. Be sure to include nonbinary as an option here.
- Always allowing students to use the restroom appropriate to their gender identity. If your school does not have gender-neutral restrooms, advocate for this change to happen. Students need to be able to use the bathroom without feeling unsafe or dysphoric. [19]

Role Models, Allies, and Safe Spaces

Teachers, principals, school counselors, school librarians, and other school staff need to make it obvious that they are allies to queer students. [20] That can look like:

- Taking a Safe Space training and displaying a sticker or poster.
- Displaying posters or flyers for LGBTQIA+ resources, hotlines, classes, and spaces.
- Becoming a faculty advisor for a GSA. [21]
- Making menstrual hygiene products available in men's and non-gendered restrooms.
- For queer school staff, being out, even in subtle ways, can make students feel safe and seen.
- Using gender-neutral examples in assignments can make nonbinary students feel valid.
- Swiftly redirecting and disciplining students using homophobic or transphobic language or bullying, including the common insult, "That's gay." [22]

- Helping students plan how to come out to parents and guardians, siblings, and friends.[23]

For Clinicians

Continuing Education

Medical and mental health providers must stay up-to-date on current terminology, health disparities and risks, sexual behaviors, and treatment standards. Concretely, this might include:

- Familiarizing yourself with the WPATH standards of care in order to best care for transgender patients.[24]
- Creating a saved Google search for LGBTQIA+ youth and your specialty.
- Going to conferences such as Gender Odyssey[25] and the Philadelphia Trans Wellness Conference[26] to access the most current standards of care.
- Learning about safer sex practices in queer and trans communities.
- Educating yourself about how queer and trans identities have been medicalized and pathologized.[27]

Resources

It's always appreciated when clinicians have resources that cater to marginalized communities' needs. Specific suggestions include the following:

- Providing queer-specific anatomy and safer sex resources to patients. This includes not just pamphlets about safer sex but also supplies such as gloves, dental dams, condoms, and lubricant. A protected community is a healthy community.
- Providing pamphlets or brochures about being queer, coming out, transition, and queer-specific healthcare.
- Having flyers or posters for queer resources such as group therapy, social and support groups, and treatments.

Forms and Records

For transgender patients, being called by their proper name and gender pronouns is not only affirming but vital for mental health. Non-heterosexual families must be included as well. This might look like:

- Updating intake and assessment forms to include patient's preferred name, gender pronouns, asking about body parts rather than biological sex, and who their partners are (again, talk about body parts rather than genders here). If you must ask about sexual orientation, include less visible orientations as well.
- Making sure you have a preferred name element in electronic records and educating staff to always use preferred name instead of legal name.
- Also having an element for gender identity, as this may be different than the gender noted on the patient's health insurance.

NOTES

FOREWORD

1. R. S. Bishop, "Mirrors, Windows, and Sliding Glass Doors," *Perspectives* 6, no. 3 (1990): ix–xi.

2. K. Kumashiro, "Queer Students of Color and Antiracist, Antiheterosexist Education: Paradoxes of Identity and Activism," *Troubling Intersections of Race and Sexuality: Queer Students of Color and Anti-Oppressive Education*, ed. K. Kumashiro, 1–25 (Lanham, MD: Rowan & Littlefield, 2001).

3. Joshua D. Safer, Eli Coleman, Jamie Feldman, Robert Garofalo, Wylie Hembree, Asa Radix, and Jae Sevelius, "Barriers to Healthcare for Transgender Individuals," *Current Opinion in Endocrinology, Diabetes and Obesity* 23, no. 2 (2016): 168–71, doi: 10.1097/MED.0000000000000227.

4. A. Rich, "Compulsory Heterosexuality and Lesbian Existence," *Signs: Journal of Women in Culture and Society* 5, no. 4 (1980): 631–60.

5. Bishop, "Mirrors, Windows, and Sliding Glass Doors."

6. S. Pennell, "Training Secondary Teachers to Support LGBTQ+ Students: Practical Applications from Theory and Research," *High School Journal* 101, no. 1 (2017): 71.

PREFACE

1. An umbrella term for sexual orientation and gender minorities. Sometimes used as a slur; now reclaimed as a politicized, non-normative identity.

2. Shortened version of "transgender." Transgender means a person who identifies as a gender different than the one they were assigned at birth, for example, somebody assigned male at birth who identifies as female.

3. Attraction to more than one gender.

4. Cisgender means identifying with the gender one was assigned at birth; non-transgender.

5. Presenting in a more masculine way. Personally, I started wearing two sports bras to squash down my chest and stopped wearing dresses and skirts.

6. Genderqueer people identify as not exclusively male or female and intentionally "queer" gender; i.e., identify or present in non-normative ways.

7. Nonbinary is an umbrella term for those who do not identify as exclusively male or female.

8. Many nonbinary people dislike the binary gendered pronouns "she" and "he" and instead use "they" and other neopronouns.

9. The process of aligning one's social, legal, and physical self with one's gender identity.

10. A compression vest that flattens breast tissue.

11. A soft phallus packed in the underwear to approximate a flaccid penis.

12. It's important to note that most trans people do not wish to discuss their transitions and it is considered very rude to inquire about them. I personally chose to share here in order to acknowledge the vulnerability of the trans participants in this study who discussed details of their transitions honestly and bravely. I am indebted to them and wish to return the favor by mirroring their vulnerability and candor.

13. An acronym that stands for lesbian, gay, bisexual, transgender, queer, intersex, asexual, plus.

1. WHAT IS QUEER ADOLESCENCE?

1. A nonbinary person who is partially aligned with the female gender.

2. A nonbinary person who is partially aligned with the male gender.

3. Genny Beemyn, "Bisexuality," *GLBTQ Encyclopedia Project*, ed. Wik Wikholm (2004), http://www.glbtqarchive.com/ssh/bisex_S.pdf.

4. Susan Stryker, "Transgender," *GLBTQ Encyclopedia Project*, ed. Wik Wikholm (2004), http://www.glbtqarchive.com/ssh/transgender_S.pdf.

5. GLAAD, "GLAAD Media Reference Guide—Lesbian/Gay/Bisexual Glossary of Terms," https://www.glaad.org/reference/lgbtq.

6. Intersex Society of North America (ISNA), "What Is Intersex?" http://www.isna.org/faq/what_is_intersex.

7. Asexual Visibility & Education Network (AVEN), "Overview," https://www.asexuality.org/?q=overview.html.

8. Partially or mostly identifying as a girl, with another gender at the same time.

9. A gender that is specific to Autistic nonbinary individuals.

10. Aaron M. White and Scott Swartzwelder, *What Are They Thinking?! The Straight Facts about the Risk-Taking, Social-Networking, Still-Developing Teen Brain* (New York: Norton, 2013), 20.

11. G. Stanley Hall, *Adolescence: Its Psychology and Its Relations to Physiology, Anthropology, Sociology, Sex, Crime, Religion, and Education*, vols. 1 and 2 (New York: Appleton, 1904).

12. A small region of the brain that releases hormones.

13. A gland in the brain that controls the function of most other endocrine glands.

14. A sex hormone responsible for the development and regulation of the reproductive system and secondary sex characteristics of people with ovaries.

15. A sex hormone responsible for the development and regulation of the reproductive system and secondary sex characteristics of people with testes.

16. A hormone produced by gonadotropic cells in the anterior pituitary gland that triggers ovulation in people with ovaries and testosterone production in people with testes.

17. A hormone produced by gonadotropic cells in the anterior pituitary gland that regulates the development, growth, pubertal maturation, and reproductive processes of the body.

18. Release of eggs from the ovaries. Jeremi M. Carswell and Diane E. J. Stafford, "Normal Physical Growth and Development," in *Handbook of Adolescent Health Care*, ed. Lawrence S. Neinstein (Philadelphia: Lippincott Williams & Wilkins, 2009), 2.

19. Armpit.

20. Carswell and Stafford, "Normal Physical Growth," 3–5.

21. Mari Radzik, Sara Sherer, and Lawrence S. Neinstein, "Psychosocial Development in Normal Adolescents," in *Handbook of Adolescent Health Care*, ed. Lawrence S. Neinstein (Philadelphia: Lippincott Williams & Wilkins, 2009), 15–16.

22. Ibid.

23. Ibid.

24. The ability to derive general rules and concepts from specific examples.

25. Radzik, Sherer, and Neinstein, "Psychosocial Development," 15–16.

26. Jeffrey Arnett, "Emerging Adulthood: A Theory of Development from the Late Teens through the Twenties," *American Psychologist* 55, no. 5 (2000): 469.

27. Ibid., 470.

28. Those who experience sexual attraction; non-asexuals.

29. Martin M. Anderson and Lawrence S. Neinstein, "Adolescent Sexuality," in *Handbook of Adolescent Health Care*, ed. Lawrence S. Neinstein (Philadelphia: Lippincott Williams & Wilkins, 2009), 357.

30. Eric Meininger and Gary Remafedi, "Gay, Lesbian, Bisexual, and Transgender Adolescents," in *Handbook of Adolescent Health Care*, ed. Lawrence S. Neinstein (Philadelphia: Lippincott Williams & Wilkins, 2009), 370.

31. D. F. Swaab, *We Are Our Brains: A Neurobiology of the Brain, from the Womb to Alzheimer's* (New York: Spiegel & Grau, 2014), 94.

32. Peter K. Smith, *Adolescence: A Very Short Introduction* (Oxford: Oxford University Press, 2016), 111.

33. Dena Phillips Swanson, Malik Chaka Edwards, and Margaret Beale Spencer, *Adolescence: Development during a Global Era* (Amsterdam: Elsevier Academic Press, 2010), 349.

34. Bertram J. Cohler and Robert M. Galatzer-Levy, *The Course of Gay and Lesbian Lives: Social and Psychoanalytic Perspectives* (Chicago: University of Chicago Press, 2000), 156.

35. Ibid., 170.

36. Anthony F. Bogaert, *Understanding Asexuality* (Lanham, MD: Rowman & Littlefield Publishers, 2012), 88.

37. Julie Sondra Decker, *The Invisible Orientation: An Introduction to Asexuality* (New York: Carrel Books, 2014), 68.

38. Amy L. Sutton, *Adolescent Health Sourcebook*, 3rd ed. (Detroit: Omnigraphics, 2010), 235.

39. Thomas E. Bevan, *The Psychobiology of Transsexualism and Transgenderism: A New View Based on Scientific Evidence* (Santa Barbara: Praeger, 2015), 138–40.

40. Aaron Devor, "Witnessing and Mirroring: A Fourteen Stage Model of Transsexual Identity Formation," *Journal of Gay & Lesbian Psychotherapy* 8, no. 1–2 (2004): 43.

41. Similar terms that are generally differentiated by desire to surgically transition (transsexual) versus an umbrella term for anybody whose gender identity does not match the assigned sex at birth (transgender).

42. Devor, "Witnessing and Mirroring," 43.

43. Testing one's internal sense of gender with the external reality of how one's friends and/or romantic partner respond to it.

44. Devor, "Witnessing and Mirroring," 43.

45. Ibid.

46. Medical personnel dismissing a trans person's lived experience and withholding medical services such as hormone replacement therapy or gender confirming surgeries.

47. Devor, "Witnessing and Mirroring," 44.

48. Heidi M. Levitt and Maria R. Ippolito, "Being Transgender: The Experience of Transgender Identity Development," *Journal of Homosexuality* (2014): 1738–40.

49. Ibid., 1743–47.

50. Ibid., 1748–53.

51. Roger J. R. Levesque, *Encyclopedia of Adolescence* (New York: Springer International, 2018), 666–67.

52. Shelley L. Craig and Lauren McInroy, "You Can Form a Part of Yourself Online: The Influence of New Media on Identity Development and Coming Out for LGBTQ Youth," *Journal of Gay & Lesbian Mental Health* 18, no. 1 (2014): 95.

53. Susan Moore and Doreen Rosenthal, *Sexuality in Adolescence: Current Trends* (London: Routledge, 2006), 129–30.

54. Cohler and Galatzer-Levy, *Course of Gay and Lesbian Lives*, 151.

55. Anne Dohrenwend, *Coming Around: Parenting Lesbian, Gay, Bisexual and Transgender Kids* (Far Hills, NJ: New Horizon Press, 2012), 105–11.

2. WHO WE ARE

1. Somebody who is attracted to people regardless of gender.

2. An asexual person who may be sexually attracted to somebody after the development of emotional or romantic attraction.

3. Being romantically (but not necessarily sexually) attracted to two or more genders.

4. An umbrella term for atypical mental, behavioral, and developmental identities including Autism.

5. A neutral or null gender, sometimes used interchangeably with agender or gender neutral.

6. Relating to women who love women.

7. A social discussion forum based on communities of interests and identities.

8. A person who experiences a range of intensity within the category "girl."

9. Partially or mostly identifying as a girl, with another gender at the same time.

10. Partially or mostly identifying as agender, with another gender at the same time.

11. A Samoan culturally specific identity meaning "in the manner of a man"; used to identify AFAB individuals who embody a masculine gender.

12. Having multiple genders.

13. Somebody who moves between genders; movement can be rapid (many times within a day) or slow (changing over months or years) or anywhere in between.

14. Anthony F. Bogaert, "Asexuality: Prevalence and Associated Factors in a National Probability Sample," *Journal of Sex Research* 41, no. 3 (2004): 279–87.

15. An asexual person who may be sexually attracted to somebody, regardless of gender, after the development of emotional or romantic attraction.

16. An aromantic person who may be slightly or occasionally romantically attracted to some people. Sometimes shortened to "gray-aro."

17. About 1 percent of people are born with some kind of intersex variation, according to the Intersex Society of North America, "How Common Is Intersex?" http://www.isna.org/faq/frequency.

18. Latinx is a gender-neutral way to refer to people whose heritage is Latin American.

3. SEX EDUCATION

1. Bex Vankoot, "This Is What Sex Ed Looks Like across the Country," *Esquire*, June 24, 2019, https://www.esquire.com/lifestyle/sex/a27663524/sex-edcuation-in-america-state-by-state-1559243998.

2. Alesha E. Doan and Deborah R. McFarlane, "Saying No to Abstinence-Only Education: An Analysis of State Decision-Making," *Publius: The Journal of Federalism* 42, no. 4 (January 2012): 613.

3. Vankoot, "This Is What Sex Ed Looks Like across the Country."

4. Windy City Media Group, "LGBTQ Inclusive Curriculum Bill Approved by Illinois Gov. JB Pritzker," *Windy City Times*, August 9, 2019, http://www.windycitymediagroup.com/lgbt/LGBTQ-Inclusive-Curriculum-Bill-Approved-by-Illinois-Gov-JB-Pritzker/66747.html.

5. Carol R. Freedman-Doan, Leanna Fortunato, Erin J. Henshaw, and Jacqueline M. Titus, "Faith-Based Sex Education Programs: What They Look Like and Who Uses Them," *Journal of Religious Health* 52 (2013): 248.

6. Joseph G. Kosciw, Emily A. Greytak, Adrian D. Zongrone, Caitlin M. Clark, and Nhan L. Truong, *The 2017 National School Climate Survey: The Experiences of Lesbian, Gay, Bisexual, Transgender, and Queer Youth in Our Nation's Schools* (New York: GLSEN, 2018), 57.

7. Karli Reeves, "Sex Education or Self Education? LGBT+ Experiences with Exclusionary Curricula (Honors Undergraduate Thesis, University of Central Florida, 2019), *Honors Undergraduate Theses*, 500, https://stars.library.ucf.edu/honorstheses/500, 36–38.

8. Centers for Disease Control and Prevention (CDC), "Health Considerations for LGBTQ Youth," https://www.cdc.gov/healthyyouth/disparities/smy.htm.

9. As of January 2018, seven states have "no promo homo" laws: Alabama, Arizona, Louisiana, Mississippi, Oklahoma, South Carolina, and Texas.

10. GLSEN, "Laws Prohibiting 'Promotion of Homosexuality' in Schools: Impacts and Implications" (Research Brief) (New York: GLSEN, 2018).

11. American College of Obstetricians and Gynecologists Committee on Adolescent Health Care, "Comprehensive Sexuality Education" (Committee Opinion No. 678) (Washington, DC: ACOG, 2016).

4. GOING THROUGH PUBERTY

1. National Child Traumatic Stress Network, "LGBTQ Youth," https://www.nctsn.org/what-is-child-trauma/populations-at-risk/lgbtq-youth.

2. Centers for Disease Control and Prevention (CDC), "LGBT Youth," https://www.cdc.gov/lgbthealth/youth.htm.

3. Differences in sex development; not fitting neatly into one or the other biological sex.

4. National Eating Disorders Association, "Eating Disorders in LGBTQ+ Populations," https://www.nationaleatingdisorders.org/learn/general-information/lgbtq.

5. Assigned female at birth.

6. Intersex Society of North America (ISNA), "What Is Intersex?" http://www.isna.org/faq/what_is_intersex.

7. Among others, see Sujita Kumar Kar, Ananya Choudhury, and Abhishek Pratap Singh, "Understanding Normal Development of Adolescent Sexuality: A Bumpy Ride," *Journal of Human Reproductive Science* 8, no. 2 (2015): 70–74.

5. PARENTAL AND PEER INVOLVEMENT

1. GLSEN, "Gay-Straight Alliances: Creating Safer Schools for LGBT Students and Their Allies" (Research Brief) (New York: GLSEN, 2007), 1.

2. Ibid., 2.

3. Thomas E. Bevan, *The Psychobiology of Transsexualism and Transgenderism: A New View Based on Scientific Evidence* (Santa Barbara: Praeger, 2015), 140.

4. Joseph G. Kosciw, Emily A. Greytak, Adrian D. Zongrone, Caitlin M. Clark, and Nhan L. Truong, *The 2017 National School Climate Survey: The Experiences of Lesbian, Gay, Bisexual, Transgender, and Queer Youth in Our Nation's Schools* (New York: GLSEN, 2018), 23.

5. Ibid., 24–26.

6. Ibid., 25.

7. All thoroughly discussed in ibid., 37–38.

6. EXPLORING GENDER

1. Roger J. R. Levesque, *Encyclopedia of Adolescence* (New York: Springer International, 2018), 1544.

2. As discussed in Shelley L. Craig and Lauren McInroy, "You Can Form a Part of Yourself Online: The Influence of New Media on Identity Development and Coming Out for LGBTQ Youth," *Journal of Gay & Lesbian Mental Health* 18, no. 1 (2014): 95–109.

3. An egg is a transgender person during the time before they realized they were transgender.

4. Female-to-male; transgender men.

5. Removal of the testicles.

6. Surgical creation of a neovagina.

7. Breast removal.

8. Removal of the ovaries.

9. Removal of the uterus.

10. Surgical creation of a neophallus.

11. Thomas E. Bevan, *The Psychobiology of Transsexualism and Transgenderism: A New View Based on Scientific Evidence* (Santa Barbara: Praeger, 2015), 158.

12. A complex construct designed to make trans people miserable, passing means appearing cis. Many trans people do not meet cis-centric standards of beauty and are "clocked" or identified as transgender by onlookers. This can make a person feel less valid in their gender.

13. Levesque, *Encyclopedia of Adolescence*, 446.

14. Eric Meininger and Gary Remafedi, "Gay, Lesbian, Bisexual, and Transgender Adolescents," in *Handbook of Adolescent Health Care*, ed. Lawrence S. Neinstein (Philadelphia: Lippincott Williams & Wilkins, 2009), 375.

15. Levesque, *Encyclopedia of Adolescence*, 668.

16. Bevan, *The Psychobiology of Transsexualism and Transgenderism*, 156.

7. EXPLORING SEXUALITY

1. Amy L. Sutton, *Adolescent Health Sourcebook*, 3rd ed. (Detroit: Omnigraphics, 2010), 235.

2. This is purely hypothetical, of course. Bisexuality specifically is still misunderstood, stereotyped, and mistrusted in many communities.

3. Anne Dohrenwend, *Coming Around: Parenting Lesbian, Gay, Bisexual and Transgender Kids* (Far Hills, NJ: New Horizon Press, 2012), 98.

4. It's a problem of labeling. Without knowledge of asexuality as an orientation, asexuals are unable to identify with the larger group of asexuals and learn about themselves. Much excellent information about labeling and identity formation can be found in Anthony F. Bogaert, *Understanding Asexuality* (Lanham, MD: Rowman & Littlefield, 2012).

5. As many as 40 percent of homeless youth identify as LGBTQ, according to Dohrenwend, *Coming Around*, 135.

6. Eric Meininger and Gary Remafedi, "Gay, Lesbian, Bisexual, and Transgender Adolescents," in *Handbook of Adolescent Health Care*, ed. Lawrence S. Neinstein (Philadelphia: Lippincott Williams & Wilkins, 2009), 371.

7. Dohrenwend, *Coming Around*, 134.

8. COMING OUT

1. Roger J. R. Levesque, *Encyclopedia of Adolescence* (New York: Springer International, 2018), 667.

2. Paula Rust, "Finding a Sexual Identity and Community: Therapeutic Implications and Cultural Assumptions in Scientific Models of Coming Out," in *Psychological Perspectives on Lesbian, Gay, and Bisexual Experiences*, ed. Linda Garnets and Douglas C. Kimmel (New York: Columbia University Press, 2003), 227. See also Michael Sadowski, *In a Queer Voice: Journeys of Resilience from Adolescence to Adulthood* (Philadelphia: Temple University Press, 2013).

3. Anne Dohrenwend, *Coming Around: Parenting Lesbian, Gay, Bisexual and Transgender Kids* (Far Hills, NJ: New Horizon Press, 2012), 96.

4. Amy L. Sutton, *Adolescent Health Sourcebook*, 3rd ed. (Detroit: Omnigraphics, 2010), 241.

5. See excellent data and analysis in Shelley L. Craig and Lauren McInroy, "You Can Form a Part of Yourself Online: The Influence of New Media on Identity Development and Coming Out for LGBTQ Youth," *Journal of Gay & Lesbian Mental Health* 18, no. 1 (2014): 95–109.

6. This was also noted in Frank J. Floyd and Roger Bakeman, "Coming-Out across the Life Course: Implications for Age and Historical Context," *Archives of Sexual Behavior* 35 (2006): 287–96. Due to recent societal openness about gender and sexual identity, youth coming out currently tend to exhibit an identity-centered pattern, as opposed to the earlier common pattern of sexual experimentation before determining one's identity.

7. In fact, it's quite rare for siblings or parents to hear first; youth typically disclose first to close friends and/or queer adult role models, according to Ellen C. Perrin, *Sexual Orientation in Child and Adolescent Health Care* (New York: Kluwer Academic, 2002), 79.

8. Sutton, *Adolescent Health Sourcebook*, 232.

9. This response is quite common and is well-documented in Julie Sondra Decker's *The Invisible Orientation: An Introduction to Asexuality* (New York: Carrel Books, 2014).

10. Which doesn't even make sense.

9. TRANSITION

1. Thomas E. Bevan, *The Psychobiology of Transsexualism and Transgenderism: A New View Based on Scientific Evidence* (Santa Barbara: Praeger, 2015), 153.

2. For detailed information about transition, please see the following resources. Hudson's FTM Resource Guide (http://www.ftmguide.org) includes information about testosterone therapy, grooming, clothing, social presentation, and surgical interventions for AFAB transgender people. Andrea James's Transgender Map (https://www.transgendermap.com) includes information about all aspects of social, legal, and medical/surgical transition for all transgender people.

3. Some medical professionals have rigid binarist beliefs about gender identity and presentation and believe that gender transition looks one very specific way. Patients who do not align with this view are sometimes misbelieved and affirming treatments are withheld. This has meant that many trans people parrot the dominant view in order to access treatment.

4. Not recommended as they can cause physical damage.

5. Gender confirmation surgery/sexual reassignment surgery.

10. WHAT WE WISH HAD BEEN DIFFERENT

1. Trans researcher Aaron Devor has much to say about the power of marginalized identities being seen truly and wholly: "Validations offered by non-transgendered friends, loved ones, co-workers, and interested professionals of the gender and sex identities of transgendered people can serve as a powerful reinforcer of transgendered identities" (46). Learn more in "Witnessing and Mirroring: A Fourteen Stage Model of Transsexual Identity Formation," *Journal of Gay & Lesbian Psychotherapy* 8, no. 1–2 (2004): 41–67.

2. J. Douglas Bremner, "Traumatic Stress: Effects on the Brain," *Dialogues in Clinical Neuroscience* 8, no. 4 (2006): 445–61.

3. For a discussion of femmephobia, see Brynn Tannehill, "6 Ways Femmephobia Is Harming LGBTQIA+ Communities," *Everyday Feminism*, February 26, 2016, https://everydayfeminism.com/2016/02/femmephobia-queer-community.

4. Queer and/or Transgender Black, Indigenous, or People of Color.

5. Transgender people who believe that being trans is a medical condition to be treated rather than a personal and social identification.

6. For another study on what transgender youth wished they had learned in sex education, see Syd Stephenson, "Transgender People on What They Wish They Had Learned in Sex Ed," *Teen Vogue*, January 2, 2020, https://www.teenvogue.com/story/transgender-people-what-they-wish-they-learned-in-sex-ed.

7. For health and healthcare disparities in rural settings, see Caitlin Cox, "Lesbian, Gay, Bisexual, and Transgender (LGBT) Healthcare in Rural Settings: An Integrative Review of the Literature" (Honors Undergraduate Thesis, University of Central Florida), 2019, *Honors Undergraduate Theses*, 503, https://stars.library.ucf.edu/honorstheses/503.

8. GLSEN, "Teaching Respect: LGBT-Inclusive Curriculum and School Climate" (Research Brief) (New York: GLSEN, 2011), 1.

9. Ibid., 2.

10. For a discussion of reaching out to LGBTQIA+ students, see Mikhaela Singleton, "K–12 Program Reaches Out to LGBTQ+ Students across the Capital Region," News 10, December 18, 2019, https://www.news10.com/news/local-news/k-12-program-reaches-out-to-lgbtq-students-across-the-capital-region. For data on school climate for LGBTQIA+ youth, see Ryan M. Kull, Emily A. Greytak, and Joseph G. Kosciw, *Supporting Safe and Healthy Schools for Lesbian, Gay, Bisexual, Transgender, and Queer Students: A National Survey of School Counselors, Social Workers, and Psychologists* (New York: GLSEN, 2019). See also Joseph G. Kosciw, Emily A. Greytak, Adrian D. Zongrone, Caitlin M. Clark, and Nhan L. Truong, *The 2017 National School*

Climate Survey: The Experiences of Lesbian, Gay, Bisexual, Transgender, and Queer Youth in Our Nation's Schools (New York: GLSEN, 2018).

11. Samantha J. Chandler, *The Value of Acknowledging Sexual Identity in Early Adolescence: Supporting Queer Youth in Middle School* (MA Thesis, Pacific Oaks College), 2005. See especially chapter 5.

12. As previously discussed, many queer youth use social media to explore their LGBTQIA+ identities, discuss and come up with new terminology, support one another, share resources, and practice coming out. See Shelley L. Craig and Lauren McInroy, "You Can Form a Part of Yourself Online: The Influence of New Media on Identity Development and Coming Out for LGBTQ Youth," *Journal of Gay & Lesbian Mental Health* 18, no. 1 (2014): 95–109 for more data and discussion.

13. Anne Dohrenwend suggests telling your child that you are glad they told you, and argues that "it's vital to accept your child and give up any desire to change them, don't give uninvited advice about their identity, take a firm stand against discrimination and hate, and get to know your child's friends and partner" (35). See *Coming Around: Parenting Lesbian, Gay, Bisexual and Transgender Kids* (Far Hills, NJ: New Horizon Press, 2012) for more excellent suggestions.

14. Recent research suggests that attempts to make transgender people cisgender can lead to suicide attempts. See Christopher Viveiros, "Study Shows Link between Conversion Therapy and Transgender Suicide Attempts," PRWeb, September 11, 2019, https://www.prweb.com/relcases/study_shows link_between_conversion_therapy_and_transgender_suicide_attempts/ prweb16558063.htm.

15. Eli Coleman, Walter Bockting, Marsha Botzer, Peggy Cohen-Kettenis, Griet DeCuypere, Jamie Feldman, Lin Fraser, et al., *Standards of Care for the Health of Transsexual, Transgender, and Gender-Nonconforming People* (World Professional Association for Transgender Health, 2012), https://www. wpath.org/publications/soc.

16. An example of queer inclusion in elementary school curriculum can be seen here: Laura Newberry, "Boys, Girls and Genders In-Between: A Classroom Lesson for Modern Third-Graders," *Los Angeles Times*, December 17, 2019, https://www.latimes.com/california/story/2019-12-17/on-the-lesson-plan-for-this-third-grade-class-gender-diversity. More excellent resources can be found in Olivia B. Waxman, "As More States Require Schools to Teach LGBTQ History, Resources for Teachers Expand," *Time*, December 13, 2019, https://time.com/5747670/lgbtq-history-resources. For even more suggestions, see John Elia and Michele Eliason, "Discourses of Exclusion: Sexuality Education's Silencing of Sexual Others," *Journal of LGBT Youth* 7 (2010): 29–48.

17. For concrete recommendations, see Sexuality Information and Education Council of the United States, *Guidelines for Comprehensive Sexuality Education: Kindergarten through 12th Grade*, 3rd ed. (National Guidelines Task Force, 2004), https://siecus.org/wp-content/uploads/2018/07/Guidelines-CSE.pdf.

18. For lesson plans and video and print resources, see GLSEN, "LGBTQ-Inclusive Sexual Health Education," https://www.glsen.org/activity/inclusive-sexual-health-education-lesbian-gay-bisexual-transgender.

19. In fact, not being able to use the appropriate restroom for their gender can lead to harming the mental and physical health of the youth. See Tanya Albert Henry, "Exclusionary Bathroom Policies Harm Transgender Students' Health," American Medical Association, December 31, 2019, https://www.ama-assn.org/delivering-care/population-care/exclusionary-bathroom-policies-harm-transgender-students-health for more information.

20. *Teen Vogue* has more suggestions from interviewees. See Nick Fiorellini, "What It's Like to Be Out as LGBTQ at School," *Teen Vogue*, September 3, 2019, https://www.teenvogue.com/story/what-its-like-to-be-out-as-lgbtq-at-school. For discussion of teacher advocacy for queer students, see Janice Kroeger and Lis Regula, "Queer Decisions in Early Childhood Teacher Education: Teachers as Advocates for Gender Non-Conforming and Sexual Minority Young Children and Families," *International Critical Childhood Policy Studies Journal* 6, no. 1 (2017): 106–21. Yet another excellent example comes from the New York City Department of Education, "Guidelines to Support Transgender and Gender Expansive Students," https://www.schools.nyc.gov/school-life/policies-for-all/guidelines-on-gender/guidelines-to-support-transgender-and-gender-expansive-students.

21. For one example of the process to get a GSA started, see Lisa A. Goldstein, "Why LGBTQ+ Education Needs to Start before High School," *them,* November 29, 2017, https://www.them.us/story/lgbtq-education-needs-to-start-before-high-school.

22. Samantha Chandler further suggests training teachers "about the impact of homophobia on all students, providing tools and tactics for how to intervene, and create more inclusive curriculum," in *The Value of Acknowledging Sexual Identity in Early Adolescence*, 79.

23. For more suggestions along these lines, see Ellen C. Perrin, *Sexual Orientation in Child and Adolescent Health Care* (New York: Kluwer Academic, 2002).

24. Coleman et al., *Standards of Care for the Health of Transsexual, Transgender, and Gender-Nonconforming People*.

25. Gender Odyssey is both an annual conference and a website with information and resources. See Gender Odyssey, http://www.genderodyssey.org.

26. The Philadelphia Trans Wellness Conference is an annual conference put on by the Mazzoni Center. See Mazzoni Center, http://transphl.org/.

27. Asexuality, for example, was medicalized after the uncoupling of sex from reproduction. The DSM-III included "inhibited sex desire," which was later renamed to "hypoactive sexual desire disorder" in 1980. And later, in 1992, the ICD-10 listed "lack or loss of sexual desire." For more information, see Anthony F. Bogaert, *Understanding Asexuality* (Lanham, MD: Rowman & Littlefield, 2012).

GLOSSARY

Ableism: The system of discrimination, exclusion, and violence against disabled people; both personal, social, and structural.

Abstinence: Choosing to abstain from sex, which can mean many different things to different people. Abstinence-only sex education discourages all sexual contact and often doesn't include STI and pregnancy prevention information.

Adolescence: A complex developmental phase with several factors. As a biological and social phenomenon, it can be defined by hormonal, physical, neurological, and behavioral changes. It is a period of change that can occur between the ages of ten and twenty-four.

AFAB: Assigned female at birth; in other words, somebody with a vulva.

Ageism: Social and structural discrimination, exclusion, and violence toward older people as well as younger people.

Agender: Genderless; lacking gender.

Allistic: Not Autistic.

Allosexism: Social and structural discrimination, exclusion, and violence toward asexual people.

Allosexual: Non-asexual; experiencing sexual attraction to other people.

Ally: A person who supports and advocates on behalf of the LGBTQIA+ community.

AMAB: Assigned male at birth; in other words, somebody with a penis.

Androgyne: A person who identifies as androgynous, either both masculine and feminine or neither.

Androsexual/androphilic: Primary sexual attraction to men and masculine people.

Anorexia: An eating disorder characterized by severely limiting food intake.

Anovulatory: A menstrual cycle in which an egg is not released.

Antiandrogen: Medication that suppresses testosterone production.

Aromantic: Aromanticism is a spectrum of romantic attraction from zero to some/occasional. Many aromantics are not romantically attracted to anybody. Some are slightly or occasionally romantically attracted to some people, and are called gray-aromantic. "Aromantic" is often shortened to "aro."

Asexual: Asexuality is a spectrum of sexual attraction from zero to some/occasional. Many asexuals are not sexually attracted to anybody. Some are slightly or occasionally attracted to some people, and are called gray-asexual. Some can be attracted to somebody, but only after the development of emotional or romantic attraction, and are called demisexual. Some may be sex-repulsed, while others may engage in partnered sexual activity in order to please a partner. Some experience no sexual libido while others do. "Asexual" is often shortened to "ace."

Assigned sex at birth: The sex a baby is assigned, most often based upon external genitalia.

Autigender: A gender that is specific to Autistic nonbinary individuals.

Autism: A neurological variation that includes repetitive behavior, social and communication differences, and sensory processing differences.

BDSM: An acronym that includes three sexual practices: bondage and discipline, dominance and submission, and sadomasochism.

Bear community: A community of gay and queer men who are big, hairy, and affectionate.

Bigender: A person who identifies simultaneously as two genders, either man and woman or other genders.

Binding: Flattening breast tissue using a special garment called a binder that compresses the chest. DIY binding techniques include using sports bras or Ace bandages, the latter of which is unsafe.

Biphobia: A social and structural system of discrimination, exclusion, and violence toward bisexual people.

BIPOC: An acronym that stands for Black, Indigenous, and People of Color. It is used instead of POC to reflect the attitudes and violence faced specifically by Black and Indigenous communities.

Biromantic: Being romantically (but not necessarily sexually) attracted to two or more genders.

Bisexual: Bisexuality can be a slippery concept. It can mean being sexually or romantically attracted to your own gender and another gender, being attracted to multiple genders, or being attracted to all genders. Some people believe that bisexuality means attraction just to women and men, preferring to use the related term "pansexual" to avoid excluding transgender people who may not fit neatly into the "man" or "woman" category. But transgender-inclusive bisexuals insist that bisexuality encompasses and includes trans people.

BlaQueer: A Black and queer community that sees these two identities as connected.

Body image: Our feelings, thoughts, and attitudes about our own bodies and other people's bodies.

Bottom surgery: A range of gender confirmation surgeries performed on the lower regions of the body: for AFAB people, hysterectomy, metoidioplasty, and phalloplasty; for AMAB people, orchiectomy and vaginoplasty.

Boyflux: A person who experiences a range of intensity within the category "boy."

Bulimia: An eating disorder characterized by bingeing and purging food.

Butch: A masculine gender expression or identity that originated within the lesbian community but now can apply to any queer or transgender person.

Cervix: The opening to the uterus.

Chlamydia: A sexually transmitted infection that can cause damage to the reproductive tract.

Circumcision: Surgical removal of the foreskin from the glans of the penis.

Cisgender: A person who identifies as the sex they were assigned at birth; non-transgender.

Cissexism: Social and structural discrimination, erasure, and violence toward transgender and gender-nonconforming people.

Cisnormativity: The positioning of cisgender identity as natural and valuable, and the presumption that everybody is cisgender unless proven otherwise.

Clitoris: Part of the external and internal AFAB genitals that is the primary source of sexual stimulation and release.

Closeted/in the closet: Not disclosing to others about one's sexual or gender identity.

Coming out of the closet: Coming out entails realizing one's sexual or gender identity and then disclosing to others. Some people are out to all in their lives while others are more strategic about whom to share with.

Condoms: A safer-sex barrier method used to prevent STI transmission during vaginal and anal intercourse and oral-penile sex, as well as to prevent pregnancy during vaginal intercourse.

Consent: Enthusiastically saying "yes" to a sexual activity and only doing that activity if all parties agree to it.

Cross-dressing: Dressing in the clothes of another sex/gender. Done by both cisgender and transgender queer and straight people. Replaces an older term, "transvestite."

Crush: An often unreciprocated feeling of attraction and idealized fantasy about another person.

Culture: The language, values, beliefs, customs, and folklore of a group of people.

Dating: A social activity between two people, possibly leading to romance or sex. Often initiated in adolescence.

Deadname: A transgender person's birth name, if they have changed their name.

Deadnaming: The act of calling a transgender person by their deadname. An act of violence.

Demiboy: Partially or mostly identifying as a boy, with another gender at the same time.

Demigender: Partially or mostly identifying as one gender while also identifying as another gender at the same time.

Demigirl: Partially or mostly identifying as a girl, with another gender at the same time.

Demiromantic: An aromantic person who may be romantically attracted to somebody after the development of sexual attraction.

Demisexual: An asexual person who may be sexually attracted to somebody after the development of emotional or romantic attraction.

Dental dams: A safer-sex barrier method used to protect from STI transmission during oral-vaginal or oral-anal sex.

Disability: A restriction or lack of ability. Can be physical, psychological, emotional, neurological, or behavioral. Disability is also a cultural category that positions disabled people as non-normative.

Down low/DL: Men who identify as straight/heterosexual but have sex with other men. Often used in communities of color.

Drag king: Cross-dressing as a man for entertainment purposes.

Drag queen: Cross-dressing as a woman for entertainment purposes.

DSG: An acronym that stands for diverse sexualities and genders.

Dyadic: Non-intersex; having characteristics associated with only one biological sex.

Dyke: A slur or reclaimed term for a lesbian.

Dysphoria: An emotional or physical feeling of intense discomfort due to social misgendering or dissonance from body parts.

Early adolescence: The period of adolescence between the ages of about ten to fifteen, which is marked by puberty and increasing independence from parents.

Early maturation: Earlier than normal pubertal maturation.

Egg: A transgender person who has not yet realized they are transgender. The moment of gender self-awareness is sometimes called "cracking the egg."

Emerging adulthood: A term coined by Jeffrey Arnett meaning the stage of life between adolescence and adulthood, a time of life when many young adults explore issues of identity.

Erasure: Diminishing or refusing as valid a sexual orientation or gender identity. For example, saying that a bisexual person is actually just gay and hasn't figured it out yet is a form of bisexual erasure.

Erotica: Erotic novels, short stories, photography, and video intended to sexually arouse; often called pornography when in visual form.

Estrogen: The hormone responsible for breast development and other secondary sexual characteristics in AFAB people. Transfeminine people who are medically transitioning take a form of estrogen called estradiol to achieve some of the same results.

Ethnicity: A cultural category based on shared national origin, language, values, politics, and history.

Fa'atane: A Samoan culturally specific identity meaning "in the manner of a man"; used to identify AFAB individuals who embody a masculine gender.

Fag/faggot: A slur or reclaimed term for a gay man.

Fatphobia: A social and structural system of discrimination, exclusion, and violence toward fat bodies.

Femme: A feminine gender expression or identity that originated in the lesbian community but now can apply to all queer and transgender people.

Follicle-stimulating hormone (FSH): A hormone produced by the pituitary gland that acts on the gonads.

FTM: Female-to-male trans person. Mostly used in older communities, as younger generations dislike the connotation that they were once female.

Gaff: A special clothing accessory that keeps the penis and testicles tucked while creating a smooth surface. Many trans people make their own using nylon stockings.

Gatekeeping: When medical and mental health providers refuse services or offer certain services with conditions because they do not deem a patient properly transgender. Also applies to social situations where a person is perceived as "not queer enough" or "not trans enough" to engage in community.

Gay: Can refer either to men or man-aligned people who are sexually or romantically attracted to other men or man-aligned people, or as a catchall for any homosexual feelings or behavior. For example, a lesbian or bisexual woman may refer to herself as gay.

Gender binary: The idea that there are only two genders, man and woman.

Gender confirmation surgery: A range of surgeries undertaken to reduce dysphoria and align the body with a person's true felt gender. Includes facial feminization surgeries, top surgeries (mastectomy or breast augmentation), and bottom surgeries (includes hysterectomy, phalloplasty, orchiectomy, vaginoplasty, and others). Also called sexual reassignment surgery, though this is a somewhat dated term.

Gender expansive: A term used to describe a person who expands and explodes traditional ideas of gender.

Gender expression: The ways in which we communicate our gender identities, through dress, grooming, gesture, gait, speech, and so forth.

Gender identity: One's felt sense of their own gender. Can include binary identities (male/man and female/woman) and nonbinary identities (genderqueer, genderfluid, and many others).

Gender nonconforming: Not conforming to rigid gender roles, expectations, and social presentation for one's assigned gender. Sometimes a concrete identity.

Gender policing: The act of discouraging non-normative gender expression, such as not letting a young boy play with a doll.

Gender pronouns: How we refer to people when they are not there. Includes he/him/his/himself, she/her/hers/herself, and they/them/themself, and others. Using the proper gender pronouns is very important to transgender people.

Gender roles: The gender expression and gendered behaviors expected of a particular gender; for example, the idea that only women work in childcare.

Gender variant: Someone who varies from traditional ideas of their assigned gender, in terms of expression, identity, or perception.

Genderfluid: Somebody who moves between genders; movement can be rapid (many times within a day) or slow (changing over months or years) or anywhere in between.

Genderflux: A person who experiences a range of intensity within a specific gender category.

Genderqueer: A person who experiences their gender as queer: non-normative, nonconforming, and political.

Genital herpes: A sexually transmitted infection caused by an incurable virus. Characterized by sores or blisters that may or may not reoccur.

Genital warts: A sexually transmitted infection caused by the human papillomavirus.

Girlflux: A person who experiences a range of intensity within the category "girl."

Glans: The part of the penis or clitoris that is most sensitive to arousal.

Gloves: A safer-sex barrier method used to protect from STI transmission, mess, and fingernail injury during manual sex.

Gonadarche: The second stage of puberty, involving testicular and ovarian enlargement. Occurs before menarche or spermarche.

Gonadotropin-releasing hormone (GnRH): A hormone produced by the hypothalamus and involved in regulating puberty timing.

Gonads: Ovaries and testes; the sex glands.

Gonorrhea: A sexually transmitted disease caused by a bacterium.

Gray-asexual: An asexual person who may be slightly or occasionally sexually attracted to some people. Sometimes shortened to "gray-ace."

Gray-aromantic: An aromantic person who may be slightly or occasionally romantically attracted to some people. Sometimes shortened to "gray-aro."

Growth spurt: A period of rapid growth in adolescents.

GSM: An acronym that stands for gender and sexual minorities.

Gynesexual/gynephilic: Primary sexual attraction to women and feminine people.

Hermaphrodite: A historic term that is now a harmful slur for intersex people. See "Intersex" for more information.

Heteronormativity: The positioning of heterosexuality as natural and valuable, and the presumption that everybody is heterosexual unless proven otherwise.

Heterosexism: A social and structural system of discrimination, exclusion, and violence toward non-heterosexual people.

Heterosexual: Straight or sexually/romantically attracted to the opposite sex.

HIV/AIDS: Acronyms that stand for human immunodeficiency virus and acquired immune deficiency syndrome, which are sexually transmitted diseases with no current cure.

Homophobia: Hatred for or fear of queer people. Manifests not just socially (bullying or violence) but also structurally (bigoted laws, medical gatekeeping, etc.).

Homosexual: A person who experiences romantic and/or sexual attraction to the same gender; also called gay. Sometimes perceived as a slur due to its medical origins.

Hormone: A chemical messenger regulated by the endocrine system.

Hormone replacement therapy: Medical treatment with cross-sex hormones to achieve feminine or masculine secondary sex characteristics. Transfeminine people generally take an antiandrogen (testosterone blocker) and estradiol (estrogen). Transmasculine people generally take testosterone.

Hymen: A fold of skin that partially covers the vagina, also called the corona. There is a popular, though inaccurate, belief that the hymen always tears away at first intercourse and is thus a sign of virginity. The truth is, the hymen often stretches rather than rips, many people do not have a hymen in the first place, and virginity is a flawed cultural construction based on devaluing girls and women.

Hypothalamus: The center within the brain that controls hormonal activity, as well as regulatory activities like eating, drinking, and body temperature.

Hysterectomy: Surgical removal of the uterus. Sometimes also includes the cervix, fallopian tubes, and/or ovaries.

Imposter syndrome: Feelings of inadequacy in one's sexual orientation or gender identity. One common manifestation is nonbinary people feeling "not trans enough."

Inclusive language: Using non-gendered language to avoid assumptions about sexual orientation, sexual orientation, and relationship types; for example, using "esteemed guests" instead of "ladies and gentlemen."

Internalized homophobia: Self-hatred for being gay, lesbian, or bisexual+.

Internalized transphobia: Self-hatred for being transgender.

Intersectionality: A term used to describe the interconnectedness of oppression systems and multiple marginalizations.

Intersex: Intersex people are those whose biological sex doesn't align strictly with the categories "male" or "female." This can include ambiguity or mixing of chromosomes, reproductive organs, sex hormones, external genitals, or secondary sex characteristics. Most intersex people are assigned a gender at birth, and most identify as that gender. Some do not and may identify as transgender. Sometimes called DSD or disorders/differences of sex development. "Hermaphrodite" is an outdated term for intersexuality that is now seen as a slur.

Invisibility: When a sexual orientation or gender identity is unseen. This can be due to relationship status or external disregard. For example, a bisexual person in an opposite-gender relationship is often viewed as just straight, and asexuals are often invisible due to a lack of widespread societal understanding.

Kink: Sexual practices and behaviors outside the "normative" range. Includes roleplay, paraphilias, BDSM, leather, and more.

Labia: Folds of skin on the vulva. Inner labia surround the opening to the vagina, and outer labia surround the inner labia and the clitoris.

Late adolescence: The period of adolescence between the ages of about sixteen to nineteen. Characterized by achieving an identity, focusing on sexual identity, vocational aspirations, and personal beliefs.

Late maturation: Later than normal pubertal maturation.

Latinx: A gender-neutral way to refer to people whose heritage is Latin American; also used by nonbinary Latin Americans to identify themselves.

Leather community: A community of people who enjoy wearing leather both in and out of erotic settings. Associated with the queer community, but not all leather community members are queer.

Lesbian: A woman or woman-aligned person who is sexually or romantically attracted to other women or woman-aligned people.

Lesbophobia: A social and structural system of discrimination, exclusion, and violence toward lesbians and queer women.

LGBTQIA+: An acronym that intends to include all gender and sexual orientation minorities underneath a neat umbrella. It stands for lesbian, gay, bisexual, transgender, queer, intersex, asexual, and the "plus" signifies that there may be myriad other identities that fit within this diverse group.

Luteinizing hormone (LH): A hormone produced by the anterior pituitary that acts on the gonads.

Man-aligned: A nonbinary person who is partially aligned with the male gender.

Masculine of center (MOC): A term used to describe lesbians, queer women, and AFAB transgender people who lean more toward masculinity.

Masturbation: Self-stimulation of the genitals.

Maturation: The process of maturing sexually; also called puberty.

Menarche: The initiation of the first menstrual period.

Menopause: The cessation of the menstrual cycle, generally in middle age.

—

Metoidioplasty: Surgical release of the clitoral hood, generally after testosterone therapy has enlarged the clitoris.

Microaggressions: Subtle but biting instances of discrimination, exclusion, or verbal violence; for example, somebody using the phrase "that's gay" to indicate something bad.

Minority: A marginalized social or cultural group.

Minority stress: Chronic stress experienced by marginalized groups. Microaggressions often contribute to minority stress.

Misgendering: When a person uses the deadname or incorrect pronoun of a transgender person or calls them the wrong gender, either accidentally or maliciously.

Monogamy: The practice of being with only one romantic/sexual partner at a time.

Monosexism: The privileging of monogamy over polyamory.

MTF: Male-to-female trans person. Mostly used in older communities, as younger generations dislike the connotation that they were once male.

MSM: Men who have sex with men; may or may not identify as gay or queer.

Multigender: Having multiple genders.

Mx.: A gender-neutral honorific; used instead of Ms., Mrs., or Mr.

Neopronouns: Novel gender pronouns used for nonbinary persons. Common ones include ze/hir/hirs/hirself, ey/em/emself, and ze/zer/zers/zerself.

Neurodiversity: The wide range of neurological, psychological, and developmental variations in humans. A person is said to be neurodiverse or neuroatypical if they have a neurological, psychological, or developmental disability.

Neuroendocrine system: A system that includes the glands that produce hormones and those parts of the nervous system that activate, inhibit, and control hormone production.

Neurotypical: The state of being neurologically, psychologically, and developmentally "normative."

Neutrois: A neutral or null gender, sometimes used interchangeably with agender or gender neutral.

Nocturnal emission: Spontaneous ejaculation during sleep; sometimes called a wet dream.

Nonbinary: Somebody who doesn't fully fit into a binary (male or female) gender. Nonbinary people can identify as a mixture of genders, fluidly move between genders, identify as a gender outside the binary, or identify as genderless.

Oophorectomy: Surgical removal of the ovaries.

Orchiectomy: Surgical removal of the testicles.

Outing: The act of disclosing somebody else's sexual orientation or gender identity without their permission. An act of violence.

Ovaries: AFAB gonads that house ova and produce sex hormones.

Ovum: An AFAB sex cell or egg produced by the ovaries; plural ova.

Packing: Using a prosthetic device to create a pelvic bulge. There are special packing dildos that are soft, or many folks use socks, condoms filled with lube, and other DIY methods.

Pansexual: A person who is sexually attracted to others regardless of gender identity. Sometimes used interchangeably with "bisexual," though some community members differentiate the two, positing that "bisexual" excludes transgender people.

Passing: The act of appearing cisgender, heterosexual, white, or any other dominant cultural group. Many transgender people wish to pass so they can live stealth.

Patriarchy: Any social system where power, authority, and control are held by mostly men.

Person with a trans history: Used by people who want to acknowledge their transgender past but no longer identify as transgender because their transition is complete.

Phalloplasty: Surgical creation of a penis.

Polyamory: The practice of having more than one romantic/sexual partner or being open to it. Some polyamorous people have a primary partner and one or more secondary (or tertiary) partners, while others do not have a hierarchy. Polyamory is different than cheating because all parties are on the same page.

Prefrontal cortex: Region of the brain (in front of the forehead) involved in abstract thought.

Prepuce: A thin skin covering the glans of the penis or clitoris.

Primary sex characteristics: Reproductive system differences between AFAB and AMAB bodies; in other words, the internal and external genitals as well as the reproductive organs.

Privilege: Benefits given to a people in a specific social category. Examples include white privilege, cisgender privilege, and heterosexual privilege.

Progesterone: A sex hormone found in higher levels in AFAB bodies that contributes to the regulation of the menstrual cycle.

Prosthetics: Items used to pad breasts, hips, buttocks, and groins.

Puberty: The stage in adolescence when the youth is able to reproduce. For AFAB bodies, this means menarche (as well as secondary sex characteristic development). For AMAB bodies, this means spermarche (as well as secondary sex characteristic development).

Puberty blockers: Sex hormone suppressing medication, used in prepubertal and adolescent children to delay puberty. After a period of exploration and growth, a youth can then decide to stop puberty blockers and initiate natal puberty or begin cross-sex hormones in order to transition.

Pubic lice: Parasitic insects that are usually sexually transmitted. Also called crabs.

QTBIPOC: An acronym that stands for queer and transgender Black, Indigenous, and People of Color.

QTPOC: An acronym that stands for queer and transgender People of Color.

Queer: Queer is an inherently politicized identity as it is a reclaimed slur. It reflects non-normativity, anti-assimilationism, and radical politics. Some people dislike the term due to its use as a derogatory word for LGBTQIA+ people. Other people use it as a catchall for all gender and sexual orientation minorities.

Questioning: Being unsure of one's gender or sexuality. Often entails exploration.

QUILTBAG: An acronym that stands for queer/questioning, undecided, intersex, lesbian, transgender, bisexual, asexual/ally, and gay.

Race: A cultural category that divides people into groups based upon physical appearance, geopolitical location, culture, history, and ethnicity.

Racism: A social and structural system of discrimination, exclusion, and violence toward marginalized racial and ethnic groups by the dominant racial group in power.

Relational aggression: Aggression by manipulating relationships, such as through gossip.

Resilience: Attitudes and social skills that enable people to function well despite hardship.

Romantic orientation: A person's romantic attraction to other people, whether homoromantic, biromantic, heteroromantic, aromantic, or other identities.

Safer sex: Methods to reduce the risks of pregnancy and STIs. Includes using condoms, dental dams, and gloves, as well as being "safe, sane, and sober."

Same-gender loving (SGL): A person who loves members of their own gender. Used predominantly by those African Americans who do not identify with the words "gay" or "lesbian."

Secondary sex characteristics: External physical differences between AFAB and AMAB bodies; in other words, facial and body hair, breast development, and male and female musculature and fat distribution patterns. Can be altered through hormone replacement therapy.

Self-esteem: An individual's positive or negative opinion about themself.

Sex: A medically constructed category based upon the physical appearance of the genitalia, as well as reproductive organs, secondary sex characteristics, hormones, and chromosomes.

Sexism: A social and structural system of discrimination, exclusion, and violence toward women, feminine people, and some AFAB transgender people.

Sexual education: Sometimes called sexuality education, reproductive health education, or sex ed. Curricula that cover sexual anatomy, menstruation, hygiene, and reproduction. Many also include information about STIs and HIV/AIDS as well as birth control and STI prevention and treatment. Some also include information about queer and trans identities, consent and healthy relationships, and negotiating pleasure.

Sexual-minority youth: Adolescents who are lesbian, gay, bisexual, pansexual, Two-Spirit, or any other non-heterosexual identity.

Sexual orientation: One's sexual and/or romantic attraction. Includes heterosexual (straight), gay, lesbian, bisexual, pansexual, asexual, Two-Spirit, and others.

Sexual reassignment surgery: A range of surgeries undertaken to reduce dysphoria and align the body with a person's true felt gender. Includes facial feminization surgeries, top surgeries (mastectomy or breast augmentation), and bottom surgeries (includes hysterectomy, phalloplasty, orchiectomy, vaginoplasty, and others). Also called gender confirmation surgery.

Sexually transmitted infection (STI): An infection spread through sexual contact. Includes chlamydia, gonorrhea, herpes, syphilis, and more.

Shaft: The part of the penis or clitoris that becomes erect when aroused.

Skoliosexual: Sexual or romantic attraction to transgender and/or nonbinary people.

Socioeconomic class: A cultural category based upon education, occupation, income, and social status.

SOGIE: An acronym that stands for sexual orientation, gender identity and expression.

Sperm: A sex cell produced by the testes.

Spermarche: Sperm production and initiation of first ejaculation.

Stealth: A transgender person who is not out as trans and passes as cisgender.

Stereotype: A generalization applied to everyone in a cultural group.

Stigma: When negative stereotypes about or institutional practices around a person or group of people separate that person or group from the larger society.

Straight: Heterosexual or sexually/romantically attracted to the opposite sex.

Stud: A Black or Latina masculine queer woman.

Syphilis: A sexually transmitted infection caused by a bacterium that progresses through several stages.

TERF: An acronym that stands for trans-exclusionary radical feminist, a small but vocal minority of feminists who reject transgender people and seek to remove them from queer and women's communities.

Testes: Gonads in the scrotum that produce sperm and testosterone.

Testosterone: The hormone responsible for facial hair development and other secondary sexual characteristics in AMAB people, present in AFAB people in smaller quantities. Transmasculine people who are medically transitioning take testosterone to achieve some of the same results.

Third Gender: A culturally accepted category of sex/gender that is neither fully male/man nor female/woman. One example is the hijra in India.

Top surgery: Chest surgeries undertaken to reduce dysphoria and align one's body with one's felt gender: for AFAB people, mastectomy and chest reshaping; for AMAB people, breast augmentation.

Tranny: A slur or reclaimed term for a transgender woman.

Transfeminine: All AMAB transgender people who identify with femininity.

Transgender: People who identify as a different gender than the gender they were assigned at birth. This can include trans men, who were assigned female at birth; trans women, who were assigned male at birth; and nonbinary people, who identify as something other than the neat categories of "man" and "woman." Often shortened to trans.

Transition: A social, legal, and medical/surgical process by which transgender people align their presentation, documentation, and bodies with their felt gender. Not all transgender people transition, and those who do often pick and choose which elements to pursue.

Transmasculine: All AFAB transgender people who identify with masculinity.

Transmisogyny: Hatred for transfeminine people, often accompanied by violence. Hatred for Black transfeminine people in particular is called transmisogynoir.

Transphobia: Hatred for or fear of transgender people. Manifests not just socially (bullying or violence) but also structurally (laws, medical gatekeeping, etc.).

Transsexual: An older term that refers to those who have surgically transitioned or wish to. Many younger members of the community dislike this term as it positions gender identity in the genitals.

Tucking: A method of reducing pelvic bulge by tucking the penis and testicles into the thigh gap, generally using a gaff or very tight underwear. Some people also tuck their testes into the inguinal canals.

Two-Spirit: A distinctly Native American, First Nations, and Native Alaskan sexual orientation and/or gender identity that defies the colonial Anglo-European sexual and gender binaries. This term is culturally specific and to be used only by members of these cultures.

Uterus: A muscular structure located inside the abdomen at the top of the vagina. It holds the fetus during pregnancy and also sheds menstrual lining during menstruation.

Vagina: A muscular tube leading from the vulva to the cervix.

Vaginoplasty: Surgical creation of a vagina and vulva.

Vulva: The external genitals of an AFAB person. Includes the labia and the external clitoris.

Woman-aligned: A nonbinary person who is partially aligned with the female gender.

Woman-loving woman (WLW): A woman who loves other women. Used predominantly by those African Americans who do not identify with the words "lesbian" or "queer."

RECOMMENDED READING

519 Church Street Community Centre. *BRAZEN: Trans Women's Safer Sex Guide*. 2013. https://qtsafersex.omeka.net/items/show/2.
  A zine for transfeminine people about sexual health, STIs, hepatitis C, HIV, and safer sex.

Aaron, Eli. *Transcending Anatomy: A Guide to Bodies and Sexuality for Partners of Trans People*. 2011. https://qtsafersex.omeka.net/items/show/20.
  A guide to help partners of trans people navigate bodies and sex.

Abrams, Mere. "LGBTQIA Safe Sex Guide." *Healthline*, July 12, 2018. https://www.healthline.com/health/lgbtqia-safe-sex-guide.
  A clear and concise guide to gender identity, sexual orientation, consent, STIs, types of sex, protection, and preventive care for LGBTQIA+ folks.

AIDS Committee of Toronto. *Women Lovin'*. 2012. https://qtsafersex.omeka.net/items/show/4.
  A trans- and BIPOC-inclusive zine for queer sapphics about sexuality and gender identity, sexual and reproductive health, and safer sex.

Barcelos, Chris. Queer and Trans Safer Sex Project. https://qtsafersex.omeka.net.
  A web archive of queer- and trans-inclusive sexual education materials, including zines, brochures, and other documents.

Barker, Meg-John, and Justin Hancock. *Enjoy Sex: How, When and If You Want To*. London: Icon Books, 2017.
A warm, engaging guide to sex and sexuality that covers bodies, sexual orientation, sexual expression, and consent. Inclusive of all bodies, all sexualities, and all genders. Would be fantastic for older teens.

Bellwether, Mira. *Fucking Trans Women*. 2010. https://qtsafersex. omeka.net/items/show/31.
An instructional zine for transfeminine people and their partners focusing on anatomy and sexual mechanics.

Bertie, Alex. *Trans Mission: My Quest to a Beard*. Boston: Little, Brown, 2019.
This engaging book is part memoir and part transition guide.

Boston Women's Health Collective. *Our Bodies, Ourselves, 40th Anniversary Edition*. New York: Simon and Schuster, 2011.
Very frank and scientific, though empathetic, descriptions of AFAB body parts and how they work, what is normal and abnormal, sexual and relationship health, pleasure, safer sex, pregnancy, abortion, labor and birth, menopause, medical problems, and issues affecting sexuality and reproductive health. This fortieth anniversary edition also includes a chapter on gender identity and sexual orientation and makes some effort to state that people with "female" anatomy may identify as men or as neither sex.

Cascade AIDS Project, Men's Prevention and Wellness Department. *A Young Males Guide to . . . An Informative Zine for Guys Who Like Guys*. 2005. http://archive.qzap.org/index.php/Detail/Object/Show/object_id/304.
An information guide for young men who like men. Topics include meth, communication, STIs, anatomy, and love.

Coalition for Positive Sexuality. *Just Say Yes*. 2008. https://qtsafersex. omeka.net/items/show/16.
A zine about safer sex, STIs, birth control, abortion, and respect for queer youth.

Connell, Sara. *Queer Sex Ed.* (Podcast and Website). https://www.queersexed.org.

A very frank podcast about queer sex, including sex with dysphoria, sex during and after transition, queer sex mechanics, kink practices, consent, sexual and reproductive healthcare, and much more. Suitable for older teens.

Corinna, Heather. *S.E.X.: The All-You-Need-to-Know Sexuality Guide to Get You through Your Teens and Twenties.* Philadelphia: Da Capo Press, 2016.

A sex-ed guide for teens and young adults ages 15–29ish. Includes information about reproductive health care, the mechanics of sex, communication, and consent. Inclusive of queer, trans, and kinky youth.

Corinna, Heather. Scarleteen. https://www.scarleteen.com.

An all-around fantastic internet resource with frequent blog posts and forums devoted to young adult sexual health and wellness. Very inclusive of queer, trans, and kinky youth.

Corinna, Heather. *Wait, What? A Comic Book Guide to Relationships, Bodies, and Growing Up.* Portland, OR: Limerence Press, 2019.

Instructional comic book about puberty, gender and sexual identity, crushes, dating, consent, and sexual activity.

Erickson-Schroth, Laura, ed. *Trans Bodies, Trans Selves: A Resource for the Transgender Community.* Oxford: Oxford University Press, 2014.

An utterly crucial resource for the trans community, this book includes information on identities, coming out, sexual health, relationships, reproduction, and medical and mental health disparities and needs.

Gonzales, Kathryn. *Trans+: Love, Sex, Romance, and Being You.* Washington, DC: American Psychological Association, 2019.

An in-depth exploration of gender identity, as well as mental and physical health, transitioning, relationships, and sex.

Gowen, L. Kris. *Sexual Decisions: The Ultimate Teen Guide*. Lanham, MD: Rowman & Littlefield, 2017.

Comprehensive text explaining bodies, sex, relationships, dating violence, and how the internet influences sex and sexuality. Queer inclusive throughout and also includes an entire chapter on sexual orientation and gender identity.

Gromko, Linda. *Where's My Book? A Guide for Transgender and Gender Non-Conforming Youth, Their Parents, & Everyone Else*. Bainbridge Books, 2015.

Highly informational guide that explains natal puberty, puberty blockers, and transition, as well as other trans-specific tips for adolescence through adulthood. Written in an accessible manner for youth just entering puberty or a little before.

Hasler, Nikol. *Sex: An Uncensored Introduction*. San Francisco: Zest Books, 2015.

A funny and frank guide to puberty, sex, and sexuality. Some gender essentialism, but includes a good chapter on sexuality and gender that demystifies things like bisexuality, asexuality, and pronouns in an accessible way for teens.

Hill-Meyer, Tobi. *Trans Sexuality: A Safe Sex Guide for Trans People and Their Partners*. Seattle: Handbasket Productions. www.handbasketproductions.com.

A zine covering transgender anatomy, mechanics of sex, and safer sex practices.

Labelle, Sophie. *Sex Ed For Everyone: Comics about Relationships, Identities and Puberty*. 2019. https://www.serioustransvibes.com/listing/723432208/sex-ed-for-everyone-comics-about.

Comics about relationships, identities, and puberty. Suitable for middle-schoolers and up.

Langford, Jo. *The Pride Guide: A Guide to Sexual and Social Health for LGBTQ Youth*. Lanham, MD: Rowman & Littlefield, 2018.

A comprehensive guide for LGBTQ tweens and teens, covering body parts, identity, coming out, dating, sex and sexual health, minority stress, family support (or not), and online and offline safety. The final chapter is for parents curious about LGBTQ identities who want to support their children.

Madansky, Cynthia, and Julie Tolenlino Wood. *Safer Sex Handbook for Lesbians*. 1993. https://qtsafersex.omeka.net/items/show/18.
An informational zine about how to prevent STI and HIV transmission between cisgender lesbian women.

Miller, Saiya, and Liza Bley. *Not Your Mother's Meatloaf: A Sex Education Comic Book*. Berkeley: Soft Skull Press, 2013.
A collection of comics by young adults about sex education, body image, safe sex, sexuality, and gender.

Mirk, Sarah. *You Do You: Figuring out Your Body, Dating, and Sexuality*. Minneapolis: Twenty-First Century Books, 2020.
A queer and trans inclusive guide to relationships, sexuality, gender identity, STIs, safer sex, reproduction, and birth control.

Moen, Erika, and Matthew Nolan. *Drawn to Sex: The Basics*. Portland, OR: Limerence Press, 2018.
Informative (though graphic) comics about barriers and testing, masturbation, and sexual mechanics. Very queer and trans inclusive.

Moon, Allison, and KD Diamond. *Girl Sex 101*. Lavergne, TN: Lunatic Ink, 2018.
A trans-inclusive lesbian sex guide with contributions from more than fifteen authors.

My Kid Is Gay: Helping Families Understand Their LGBTQ Kids. 2019. https://www.mykidisgay.com.
A resource website devoted to helping parents understand and advocate for their LGBTQIA+ youth.

Owl and Fox Fisher. *Trans Teen Survival Guide*. Philadelphia: Jessica Kingsley, 2019.
An instructional guide for transgender youth about coming out and transitioning.

Palmisano, Bianca. *Safer Sex for Trans Bodies*. Whitman-Walker Health. https://www.whitman-walker.org/Guides%20PDF/Safer%20Sex%20for%20Trans%20Bodies.pdf.

A safer sex guide for transgender and gender-expansive people and their partners. Includes information on STIs and their prevention, as well as accessible information about sex during and after transition, consent, communication, and pleasure.

Pardes, Bronwen. *Doing It Right: Making Smart, Safe, and Satisfying Choices about Sex*. New York: Simon Pulse, 2013.

A basic primer on anatomy, sexual health and pleasure, and STI and pregnancy prevention. Includes a chapter on queer sexualities and one on transgender and intersex identities.

Peer Advocacy Network for the Sexual Health of Trans Masculinities. Grunt: Keep It Safe | Keep It Hot | Trans Men into Men. http://www.grunt.org.au.

A site for trans men who have sex with other (cis and/or trans) men about safer sex, negotiating pleasure, and STI/HIV testing and treatment.

Potter, Mary, Leah Newbold, and Adriana. *A Queersafe Zine*. http://archive.qzap.org/index.php/Detail/Object/Show/object_id/352.

An inclusive zine about activism, consent, STIs, HIV/AIDS, safer sex, and sex work.

Rayne, Karen. *Girl: Love, Sex, Romance, and Being You*. Washington, DC: Magination Press, 2017.

Inclusive to all self-identified girls, this sex ed book covers gender and sexual identity, dating and romance, relationships, and sex.

Sexuality Information and Education Council of the United States. *Guidelines for Comprehensive Sexuality Education: Kindergarten through 12th Grade*. 3rd ed. National Guidelines Task Force, 2004. https://siecus.org/wp-content/uploads/2018/07/Guidelines-CSE.pdf.

Detailed guidelines for K–12 educators about comprehensive and inclusive sexual education.

Silverberg, Cory, and Fiona Smyth (Illustrator). *Sex Is a Funny Word: A Book about Bodies, Feelings, and YOU*. New York: Seven Stories Press, 2015.

A beautifully illustrated comic book for kids ages 7–10 about body parts, gender, sexuality, feelings, and dating. Language is very inclusive so every kid will find something relevant to them. Age appropriate; the only sexual act mentioned is masturbation.

Silverberg, Cory, and Fiona Smyth (Illustrator). *What Makes a Baby*. New York: Seven Stories Press, 2012.

A gorgeous picture book for preschool and early elementary kids about reproduction and gestation, written so it's relevant to "every kind of family and every kind of kid." Extremely inclusive language; parents reading with their children fill in the details of their own unique story.

Smart Tart Press. *Smart Tart: A Sex Positive Zine on Sexual Health for Women, Queer, and Trans People*. https://qtsafersex.omeka.net/items/show/9.

A sex-positive zine about sexual health promotion for women, transgender and queer people. Topics include consent, structural violence, access to care, STIs, safer sex, gender identity, and sexual orientation.

Smiler, Andrew P. *Dating and Sex: A Guide for the 21st Century Teen Boy*. Washington, DC: Magination Press, 2016.

A frank and accessible guide to relationships, sex, sexuality, and puberty for teen boys. Doesn't assume that a partner will be female and has a good chapter on sexual orientation and gender roles that explains the gender and sexual binaries and how they are used to bully people.

Teen Health Source. "Queering Sexual Education." http://teenhealthsource.com/blog/queering-sexual-education.

A collection of sex ed articles and videos for LGBTQIA+ youth; a collaboration between Planned Parenthood Toronto and local queer youth. Topics include language and definitions, queer identities, consent, body positivity, sex, and healthcare.

Trevor Project. *Coming Out: A Handbook for LGBTQ Young People.* 2019.   https://www.thetrevorproject.org/wp-content/uploads/2019/10/ Coming-Out-Handbook.pdf.

Informational guide for LGBTQIA+ youth. Topics include gender identity, sexual orientation, coming out, healthy relationships, and self-care.

Witton, Hannah. *Doing It! Let's Talk about Sex.* Naperville, IL: Source-books Fire, 2018.

Accessible introduction to healthy relationships, consent, queer and trans identities, STIs, and safer sex.

BIBLIOGRAPHY

American College of Obstetricians and Gynecologists Committee on Adolescent Health Care. "Comprehensive Sexuality Education" (Committee Opinion No. 678). Washington, DC: ACOG, 2016.

Anderson, Martin M., and Lawrence S. Neinstein. "Adolescent Sexuality." In *Handbook of Adolescent Health Care*, edited by Lawrence S. Neinstein, 357–69. Philadelphia: Lippincott Williams & Wilkins, 2009.

Arnett, Jeffrey. "Emerging Adulthood: A Theory of Development from the Late Teens through the Twenties." *American Psychologist* 55, no. 5 (2000): 469–80.

Asexual Visibility & Education Network (AVEN). "Overview." https://www.asexuality.org/?q=overview.html.

Beemyn, Genny. "Bisexuality." In *GLBTQ Encyclopedia Project*, edited by Wik Wikholm. 2004. http://www.glbtqarchive.com/ssh/bisex_S.pdf.

Bevan, Thomas E. *The Psychobiology of Transsexualism and Transgenderism: A New View Based on Scientific Evidence*. Santa Barbara: Praeger, 2015.

Bogaert, Anthony F. "Asexuality: Prevalence and Associated Factors in a National Probability Sample." *Journal of Sex Research* 41, no. 3 (2004): 279–87.

———. *Understanding Asexuality*. Lanham, MD: Rowman & Littlefield, 2012.

Bremner, J. Douglas. "Traumatic Stress: Effects on the Brain." *Dialogues in Clinical Neuroscience* 8, no. 4 (2006): 445–61.

Carswell, Jeremi M., and Diane E. J. Stafford. "Normal Physical Growth and Development." In *Handbook of Adolescent Health Care*, edited by Lawrence S. Neinstein, 1–13. Philadelphia: Lippincott Williams & Wilkins, 2009.

Centers for Disease Control and Prevention (CDC). "Health Considerations for LGBTQ Youth." https://www.cdc.gov/healthyyouth/disparities/smy.htm.

———. "LGBT Youth." https://www.cdc.gov/lgbthealth/youth.htm.

Chandler, Samantha J. *The Value of Acknowledging Sexual Identity in Early Adolescence: Supporting Queer Youth in Middle School*. MA Thesis, Pacific Oaks College, 2005.

Cohler, Bertram J., and Robert M. Galatzer-Levy. *The Course of Gay and Lesbian Lives: Social and Psychoanalytic Perspectives*. Chicago: University of Chicago Press, 2000.

Coleman, Eli, Walter Bockting, Marsha Botzer, Peggy Cohen-Kettenis, Griet DeCuypere, Jamie Feldman, Lin Fraser, et al. *Standards of Care for the Health of Transsexual, Transgender, and Gender-Nonconforming People*. World Professional Association for Transgender Health, 2012. https://www.wpath.org/publications/soc.

Cox, Caitlin. "Lesbian, Gay, Bisexual, and Transgender (LGBT) Healthcare in Rural Settings: An Integrative Review of the Literature." Honors Undergraduate Thesis, University of Central Florida, 2019. *Honors Undergraduate Theses* 503. https://stars.library.ucf.edu/honorstheses/503.

Craig, Shelley L., and Lauren McInroy. "You Can Form a Part of Yourself Online: The Influence of New Media on Identity Development and Coming Out for LGBTQ Youth." *Journal of Gay & Lesbian Mental Health* 18, no. 1 (2014): 95–109.

Decker, Julie Sondra. *The Invisible Orientation: An Introduction to Asexuality*. New York: Carrel Books, 2014.

Devor, Aaron. "Witnessing and Mirroring: A Fourteen Stage Model of Transsexual Identity Formation." *Journal of Gay & Lesbian Psychotherapy* 8, no. 1–2 (2004): 41–67.

Doan, Alesha E., and Deborah R. McFarlane. "Saying No to Abstinence-Only Education: An Analysis of State Decision-Making." *Publius: The Journal of Federalism* 42, no. 4 (January 2012): 613–35.

Dohrenwend, Anne. *Coming Around: Parenting Lesbian, Gay, Bisexual and Transgender Kids*. Far Hills, NJ: New Horizon Press, 2012.

Elia, John, and Michele Eliason. "Discourses of Exclusion: Sexuality Education's Silencing of Sexual Others." *Journal of LGBT Youth* 7 (2010): 29–48.

Eveleth, Rose. "Simply Having a Gay Straight Alliance Reduces Suicide Risk for All Students." *Smithsonian*, January 23, 2014. https://www.smithsonianmag.com/smart-news/simply-having-gay-straight-alliance-reduces-suicide-risk-all-students-180949462.

Fahs, Breanne. "Daddy's Little Girls: On the Perils of Chastity Clubs, Purity Balls, and Ritualized Abstinence." *Frontiers: A Journal of Women Studies* 31, no. 3 (2010): 116–42.

Fenway Health. "New Study Shows Association between Attempts to Make Transgender People Cisgender and Suicide Attempts." https://fenwayhealth.org/new-study-shows-association-between-attempts-to-make-transgender-people-cisgender-and-suicide-attempts.

Fiorellini, Nick. "What It's Like to Be Out as LGBTQ at School." *Teen Vogue*, September 3, 2019. https://www.teenvogue.com/story/what-its-like-to-be-out-as-lgbtq-at-school.

Floyd, Frank J., and Roger Bakeman. "Coming-Out across the Life Course: Implications for Age and Historical Context." *Archives of Sexual Behavior* 35 (2006): 287–96.

Freedman-Doan, Carol R., Leanna Fortunato, Erin J. Henshaw, and Jacqueline M. Titus. "Faith-Based Sex Education Programs: What They Look Like and Who Uses Them." *Journal of Religious Health* 52 (2013): 247–62.

Gender Dysphoria Affirmative Working Group (GDA). "The Gender Affirmative Model." https://www.gdaworkinggroup.com.

Gender Spectrum. "Principles of Gender-Inclusive Puberty and Health Education." 2019. https://www.genderspectrum.org/staging/wp-content/uploads/2019/02/GenderSpectrum_2019_report_WEB_final.pdf.

GLAAD. "GLAAD Media Reference Guide—Lesbian/Gay/Bisexual Glossary of Terms." https://www.glaad.org/reference/lgbtq.

GLSEN. "Gay-Straight Alliances: Creating Safer Schools for LGBT Students and Their Allies" (Research Brief). New York: GLSEN, 2007. https://www.glsen.org/research/reports-and-briefs.

———. "Laws Prohibiting 'Promotion of Homosexuality' in Schools: Impacts and Implications" (Research Brief). New York: GLSEN, 2018. https://www.glsen.org/research/reports-and-briefs.

———. "LGBTQ-Inclusive Sexual Health Education." https://www.glsen.org/activity/inclusive-sexual-health-education-lesbian-gay-bisexual-transgender.

———. "Teaching Respect: LGBT-Inclusive Curriculum and School Climate" (Research Brief). New York: GLSEN, 2011. https://www.glsen.org/research/reports-and-briefs.

Goldstein, Lisa A. "Why LGBTQ+ Education Needs to Start before High School." *them*, November 29, 2017. https://www.them.us/story/lgbtq-education-needs-to-start-before-high-school.

Hall, G. Stanley. *Adolescence: Its Psychology and Its Relations to Physiology, Anthropology, Sociology, Sex, Crime, Religion, and Education*, vols. 1 and 2. New York: Appleton, 1904.

Henry, Tanya Albert. "Exclusionary Bathroom Policies Harm Transgender Students' Health." American Medical Association, December 31, 2019. https://www.ama-assn.org/

delivering-care/population-care/exclusionary-bathroom-policies-harm-transgender-students-health.

Hudson. Hudson's FTM Resource Guide. http://www.ftmguide.org.

Intersex Society of North America (ISNA). "What Is Intersex?" http://www.isna.org/faq/what_is_intersex.

James, Andrea. "Transgender Map." https://www.transgendermap.com.

Kar, Sujita Kumar, Ananya Choudhury, and Abhishek Pratap Singh. "Understanding Normal Development of Adolescent Sexuality: A Bumpy Ride." *Journal of Human Reproductive Science* 8, no. 2 (2015): 70–74.

Kosciw, Joseph G., Emily A. Greytak, Adrian D. Zongrone, Caitlin M. Clark, and Nhan L. Truong. *The 2017 National School Climate Survey: The Experiences of Lesbian, Gay, Bisexual, Transgender, and Queer Youth in Our Nation's Schools*. New York: GLSEN, 2018.

Kroeger, Janice, and Lis Regula. "Queer Decisions in Early Childhood Teacher Education: Teachers as Advocates for Gender Non-Conforming and Sexual Minority Young Children and Families." *International Critical Childhood Policy Studies Journal* 6, no. 1 (2017): 106–21.

Kull, Ryan M., Emily A. Greytak, and Joseph G. Kosciw. *Supporting Safe and Healthy Schools for Lesbian, Gay, Bisexual, Transgender, and Queer Students: A National Survey of School Counselors, Social Workers, and Psychologists*. New York: GLSEN, 2019.

Levesque, Roger J. R. *Encyclopedia of Adolescence*. New York: Springer International, 2018.

Levitt, Heidi M., and Maria R. Ippolito. "Being Transgender: The Experience of Transgender Identity Development." *Journal of Homosexuality* (2014): 1727–58.

Maroney, Meredith, Emmie Matsuno, Samantha LaMartine, Abby Nissenbaum, Sean Rose, J. Stewart, Mary Guerrant, Taymy Caso, Elyssa Berney, and Juan Pantoja-Patiño. "A Guide for Supporting Trans and Gender Diverse Students" (APA Report). APAGS Committee on Sexual Orientation and Gender Diversity, August 2019.

Meininger, Eric, and Gary Remafedi. "Gay, Lesbian, Bisexual, and Transgender Adolescents." In *Handbook of Adolescent Health Care*, edited by Lawrence S. Neinstein, 370–76. Philadelphia: Lippincott Williams & Wilkins, 2009.

Moore, Susan, and Doreen Rosenthal. *Sexuality in Adolescence: Current Trends*. London: Routledge, 2006.

My Kid is Gay: Helping Families Understand Their LGBTQ Kids. https://www.mykidisgay.com.

National Child Traumatic Stress Network. "LGBTQ Youth." https://www.nctsn.org/what-is-child-trauma/populations-at-risk/lgbtq-youth.

National Eating Disorders Association. "Eating Disorders in LGBTQ+ Populations." https://www.nationaleatingdisorders.org/learn/general-information/lgbtq.

New York City Department of Education. "Guidelines to Support Transgender and Gender Expansive Students." https://www.schools.nyc.gov/school-life/policies-for-all/guidelines-on-gender/guidelines-to-support-transgender-and-gender-expansive-students.

Newberry, Laura. "Boys, Girls and Genders In-Between: A Classroom Lesson for Modern Third-Graders." *Los Angeles Times*, December 17, 2019. https://www.latimes.com/california/story/2019-12-17/on-the-lesson-plan-for-this-third-grade-class-gender-diversity.

Perrin, Ellen C. *Sexual Orientation in Child and Adolescent Health Care*. New York: Kluwer Academic, 2002.

Radzik, Mari, Sara Sherer, and Lawrence S. Neinstein. "Psychosocial Development in Normal Adolescents." In *Handbook of Adolescent Health Care*, edited by Lawrence S. Neinstein, 14–17. Philadelphia: Lippincott Williams & Wilkins, 2009.

Reeves, Karli. "Sex Education or Self Education? LGBT+ Experiences with Exclusionary Curricula." Honors Undergraduate Thesis, University of Central Florida, 2019. *Honors Undergraduate Theses*, 500. https://stars.library.ucf.edu/honorstheses/500.

Russell, Stephen T., A. M. Pollitt, G. Li, and A. H. Grossman. "Chosen Name Use Is Linked to Reduced Depressive Symptoms, Suicidal Ideation, and Suicidal Behavior Among Transgender Youth." *Journal of Adolescent Health* 63, no. 4 (October 2018): 503–505.

Rust, Paula. "Finding a Sexual Identity and Community: Therapeutic Implications and Cultural Assumptions in Scientific Models of Coming Out." In *Psychological Perspectives on Lesbian, Gay, and Bisexual Experiences*, edited by Linda Garnets and Douglas C. Kimmel, 227–69. New York: Columbia University Press, 2003.

Sadowski, Michael. *In a Queer Voice: Journeys of Resilience from Adolescence to Adulthood.* Philadelphia: Temple University Press, 2013.

Safer, Joshua D., and Vin Tangpricha. "Care of the Transgender Patient." *Annals of Internal Medicine* 171, no. 1 (2019): ITC1–ITC16. doi:10.7326/AITC201907020.

Sexuality Information and Education Council of the United States. *Guidelines for Comprehensive Sexuality Education: Kindergarten through 12th Grade.* 3rd ed. National Guidelines Task Force. Washington, D.C., 2004.

Singleton, Mikhaela. "K–12 Program Reaches out to LGBTQ+ Students across the Capital Region." News 10, December 18, 2019. https://www.news10.com/news/local-news/k-12-program-reaches-out-to-lgbtq-students-across-the-capital-region.

Smith, Peter K. *Adolescence: A Very Short Introduction.* Oxford: Oxford University Press, 2016.

Stephenson, Syd. "Transgender People on What They Wish They Had Learned in Sex Ed." *Teen Vogue*, January 2, 2020. https://www.teenvogue.com/story/transgender-people-what-they-wish-they-learned-in-sex-ed.

Stonefish, Twiladawn, and Kathryn D. Lafreniere. "Embracing Diversity: The Dual Role of Gay–Straight Alliances." *Canadian Journal of Education/Revue canadienne de l'éducation* 38, no. 4 (2015): 1–27.

Stryker, Susan. "Transgender." In *GLBTQ Encyclopedia Project*, edited by Wik Wikholm. 2004. http://www.glbtqarchive.com/ssh/transgender_S.pdf.

Sutton, Amy L. *Adolescent Health Sourcebook.* 3rd ed. Detroit: Omnigraphics, 2010.

Swaab, D. F. *We Are Our Brains: A Neurobiology of the Brain, from the Womb to Alzheimer's.* New York: Spiegel & Grau, 2014.

Swanson, Dena Phillips, Malik Chaka Edwards, and Margaret Beale Spencer. *Adolescence: Development during a Global Era.* Amsterdam: Elsevier Academic Press, 2010.

Tannehill, Brynn. "6 Ways Femmephobia Is Harming LGBTQIA+ Communities." *Everyday Feminism*, February 26, 2016. https://everydayfeminism.com/2016/02/femmephobia-queer-community.

Trevor Project. *Coming Out: A Handbook for LGBTQ Young People.* 2019. https://www.thetrevorproject.org/wp-content/uploads/2019/10/Coming-Out-Handbook.pdf.

Vankoot, Bex. "This Is What Sex Ed Looks Like across the Country." *Esquire*, June 24, 2019. https://www.esquire.com/lifestyle/sex/a27663524/sex-edcuation-in-america-state-by-state-1559243998.

Viveiros, Christopher. "Study Shows Link between Conversion Therapy and Transgender Suicide Attempts." PRWeb, September 11, 2019. https://www.prweb.com/releases/study_shows_link_between_conversion_therapy_and_transgender_suicide_attempts/prweb16558063.htm.

W., Sam. "Scarleteen Confidential: Parenting Gender-Nonconforming Youth." *Scarleteen*, January 28, 2015. https://www.scarleteen.com/blog/sam_w/2015/01/28/scarleteen_confidential_parenting_gender_nonconforming_youth.

Waxman, Olivia B. "As More States Require Schools to Teach LGBTQ History, Resources for Teachers Expand." *Time*, December 13, 2019. https://time.com/5747670/lgbtq-history-resources.

White, Aaron M., and Scott Swartzwelder. *What Are They Thinking?! The Straight Facts about the Risk-Taking, Social-Networking, Still-Developing Teen Brain.* New York: Norton, 2013.

Windy City Media Group. "LGBTQ Inclusive Curriculum Bill Approved by Illinois Gov. JB Pritzker." *Windy City Times*, August 9, 2019. http://www.windycitymediagroup.com/lgbt/LGBTQ-Inclusive-Curriculum-Bill-Approved-by-Illinois-Gov-JB-Pritzker/66747.html.

INDEX

ABOUT THE AUTHOR

Charlie McNabb is a librarian, ethnographer, artist, and activist. They hold a bachelor of arts with a focus in cultural anthropology from the Evergreen State College, a master of arts in folklore from the University of Oregon, and a master of library and information science from San Jose State University. They have been a cultural consultant and archivist since 2011, providing cultural competency training and research support to faculty, students, nonprofits, and corporations. In addition, they have worked as a social sciences librarian, assisting students and faculty with research and scholarship.

Charlie is the author of *Nonbinary Gender Identities: History, Culture, Resources* and has been deeply involved with research and activism in queer communities for more than twenty years. Their research focuses on nonbinary identities and experiences, queer and trans reproductive health, and disability justice. They run a DIY archive, which you can learn more about at mcnabbarchives.wordpress.com. They also review queer media at beyondhankycode.wordpress.com and do consulting work at charliemcnabb.com.